My Morning View

"It's amazing how a mug of coffee in a landscape, with a dog or a cat, in a still life, with a simple iPhone camera, and a photographer and journalist like Tammy can tell a day-to-day story that helps heal grief. This lovely little book tells that story and you will not want to set it down until you have completely gone through it."

—Kent Griswold, author and founder of the *Tiny House Blog*

"The images from My Morning View are a demonstration of love and healing. Tammy's tender soul is revealed on each page. Use this book to create your own photography project and healing journey."

—Courtney Carver, blogger and author of *Mini-missions for Simplicity*

"The simple pleasures in life are the best, and Tammy Strobel knows that as no other. That's why we love her book, her blog, and her Instagram account. Tammy's daily posts remind us we don't need all the stuff cluttering our homes. We don't really need the latest phones and designer bags. All we need is a cup of coffee and a nice morning view."

—Flow Magazine

"As someone who also worked through bereavement by taking photographs every day, I can attest to how much healing (and personal revelation) can be found in this transformative practice. Tammy's book is a package of joy, reminding us again and again to pay attention to the smallest miracles and the simplest wonders. Life is beautiful, even during the most challenging storms."

—Susannah Conway, photographer and author of *THIS I KNOW: Notes on Unraveling the Heart*

MY MORNING VIEW

An iPhone Photography Project about Gratitude, Grief & Good Coffee

by Tammy Strobel

ISBN-10: 1941142044
ISBN-13: 978-1-941142-04-2

In loving memory of Mahlon

Beloved father and friend

You are loved

You are missed

And I know you've walked into the light

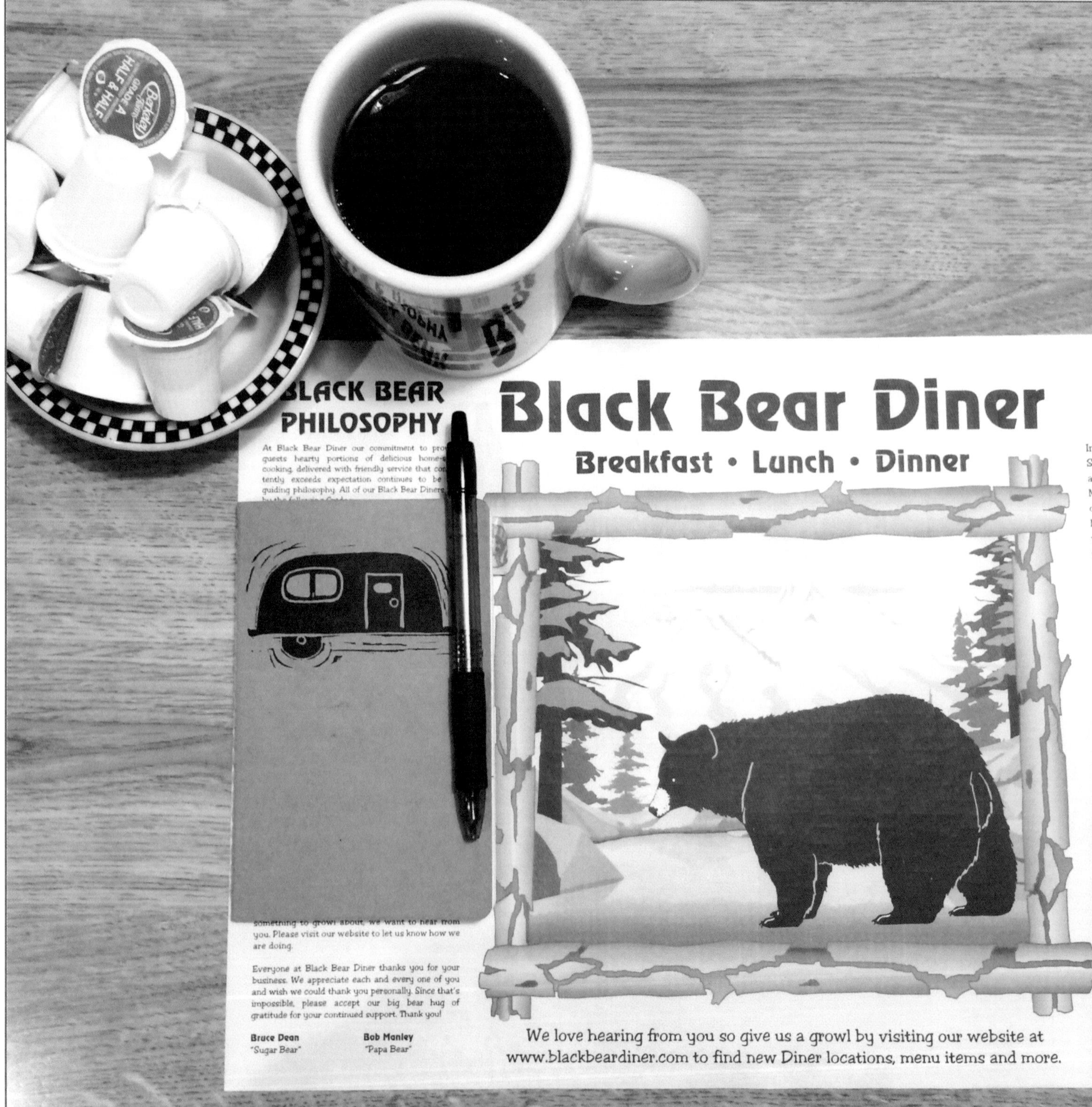

HALF & HALF
GRADE A
BLACK BEAR PHILOSOPHY
Black Bear Diner
Breakfast • Lunch • Dinner
you. Please visit our website to let us know how we are doing.
Everyone at Black Bear Diner thanks you for your business. We appreciate each and every one of you and wish we could thank you personally. Since that's impossible, please accept our big bear hug of gratitude for your continued support. Thank you!
Bruce Dean
"Sugar Bear"
Bob Manley
"Papa Bear"
We love hearing from you so give us a growl by visiting our website at
www.blackbeardiner.com to find new Diner locations, menu items and more.

CONTENTS

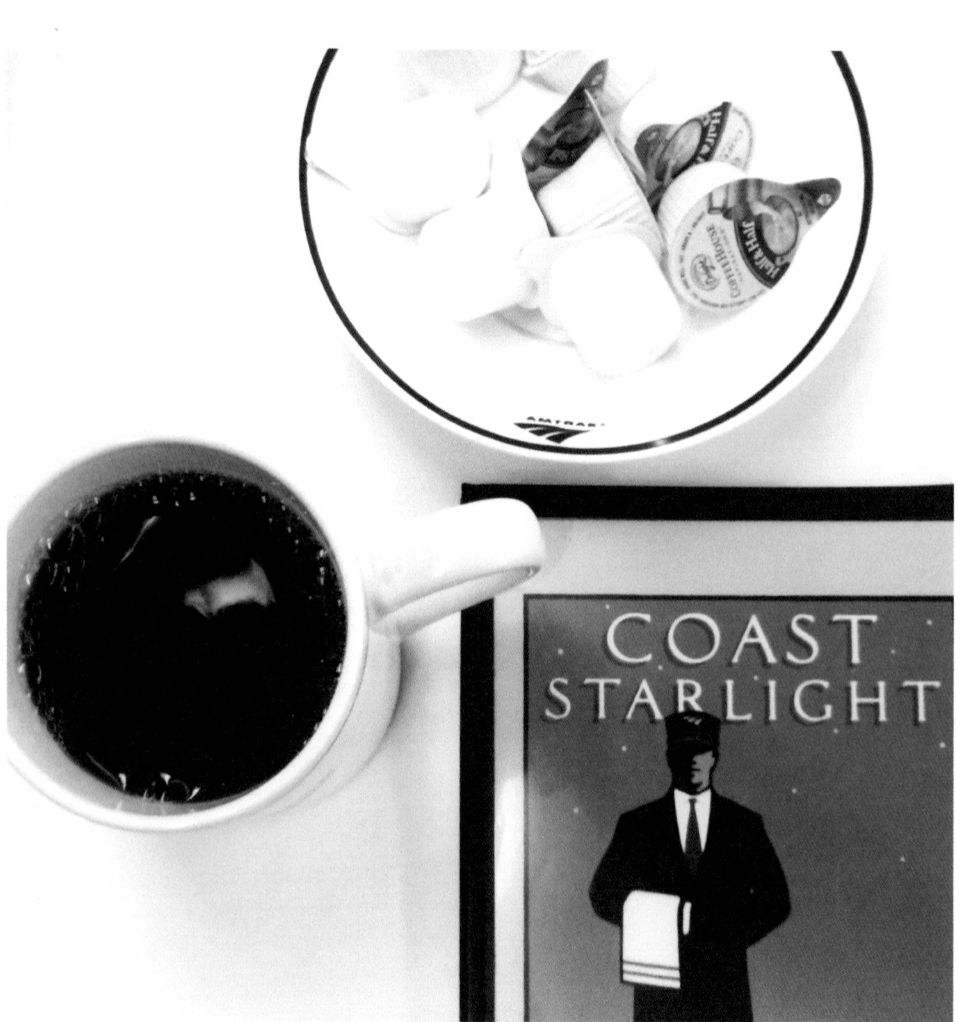
COAST
STARLIGHT

INTRODUCTION

My grief is tremendous, but my love is bigger. So is yours.

— Cheryl Strayed

On Saturday, January 14, 2012 at 7:38 a.m., I received a phone call that changed my life. The person on the other end of the line was my mom. She explained that my step-dad, Mahlon, had been airlifted to a hospital in Chico, California, and he was in the intensive care unit.

In the early morning hours, she had found Mahlon lying on the floor beside their bed. She knew Mahlon had a stroke because his speech was mumbled and he couldn't move the left side of his body. My mom called 911 immediately and waited for the emergency personnel to arrive.

As I listened to my mom explain the situation, I felt utterly terrified. Deep in my core, I knew that we were going to lose Mahlon. He already had many compounding health problems—including Parkinson's disease and the beginning stages of dementia—and intuitively I knew a stroke would complicate his fragile state.

Less than six months later, on Sunday, June 10, 2012, I found myself in a hospital room with my mom and Mahlon. My mom and I sat on the opposite sides of Mahlon's hospital bed, holding his hands and talking to him. I told Mahlon how much I loved him, that he was the best dad in the world, and that I would take care of Mom. I told him that he shouldn't worry, and it was okay to leave us behind.

I remember Leslie, Mahlon's nurse, coming into the room at 3:15 a.m. and closing the blue curtain to give us privacy. I thought to myself, "Oh, it's close. They know."

I held Mahlon's hand and gently stroked his forehead and cheeks. His cheeks were cold, and the span between his breaths kept getting longer. I kept glancing at the big, white clock and noted the time between each breath—five seconds, seven, ten, fifteen—and then he took his last, long, deep breath at 3:29 a.m. The clocked ticked on, yet Mahlon's chest was no longer moving up and down. Holding Mahlon's hand as he took his last breath was one of the hardest things I've ever done.

* * *

I miss Mahlon. I miss his laugh, I miss his smile, and I miss talking to him on the phone. I still have impulses to call him and share a story or tell him how much I love him. I'll stand there, phone in hand, and realize that my impulse can't be satisfied. Mahlon is gone, and I can't call to catch up.

After Mahlon died, everything in my life changed. I had a hard time adjusting and felt incredibly depressed and sad. I knew Mahlon would want me to keep living, to keep creating, and to stay healthy. To cope with my grief and depression, I started going on long walks. Walking has always given me solace and clarity of thought. However, focusing my attention inward on those walks was painful. I kept thinking about how much I missed Mahlon and my heart hurt. To focus my attention outward, I started bringing my camera and taking photos on my walks.

I've been taking photographs since I was ten years old. However, I didn't get serious about photography until my early twenties. At that point, I began sharing my work on my blog. Over the years, the practice of taking photos has helped me slow down, practice gratitude, and capture memories. After Mahlon's death, photography helped me heal. I wasn't ready to write about loss in a narrative form, but I could express my emotions—and honor Mahlon's memory—through my camera lens.

Mahlon loved coffee and the great outdoors. Since he was such a big influence on me, I also grew to love coffee and nature. In December 2012, I took a long walk and came home with a new idea. I decided to start an iPhone photography project on January 1, 2013 that included two things Mahlon and I loved: coffee and the great outdoors. I called the project *My Morning View.*

Each day I would climb out of bed, get dressed, make coffee, and then head outside with camera and coffee in hand. On bitterly cold days, I stayed inside and captured views within my tiny home. I would take a photo of my view, with my coffee cup in the frame, and share the image on Instagram and Facebook.

When I started this project, I didn't intend to create a photography book. My core desire was to engage in a daily habit that would help me be creative, positive, and grateful. It's my hope that this book will inspire you to pursue creative projects, even when everything in your world seems to be falling apart.

In this book you'll find a curated selection of my best photos from *My Morning View* photography series. Each photo is paired with a story, quote, or photography tip. At the end of this book, I offer a brief guide to help you begin your own daily photography project.

During 2013, I took thousands of photos and consumed countless cups of coffee. I've had so much fun with this project, and I was surprised to find it helped me heal from depression and grief. Grief is a tricky thing. On one hand, grief is painful. But grief has also given me so many gifts, including an intense appreciation for my loved ones and gratitude for tiny beautiful moments, like a long walk, my very first sip of coffee in the morning, and the stunning colors that light up Mt. Shasta. It can be challenging to notice beauty when life is hard or when you experience heart-wrenching grief. However, I have learned that when I am present and notice what's around me, I can always find beauty in my everyday life.

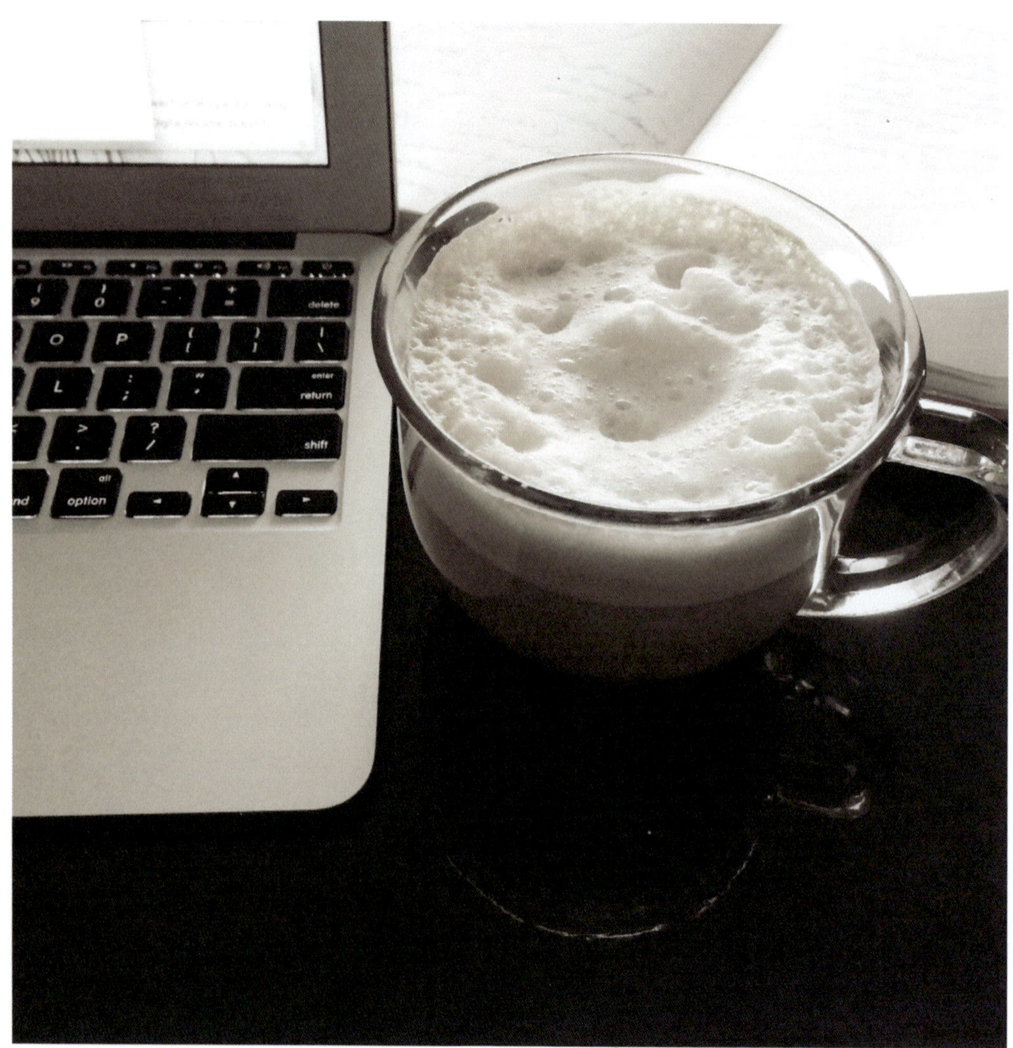
delete
enter
return
shift
alt
option

PHOTOGRAPHY

"Certain things catch your eye, but pursue only those that capture the heart."

— Native American Proverb

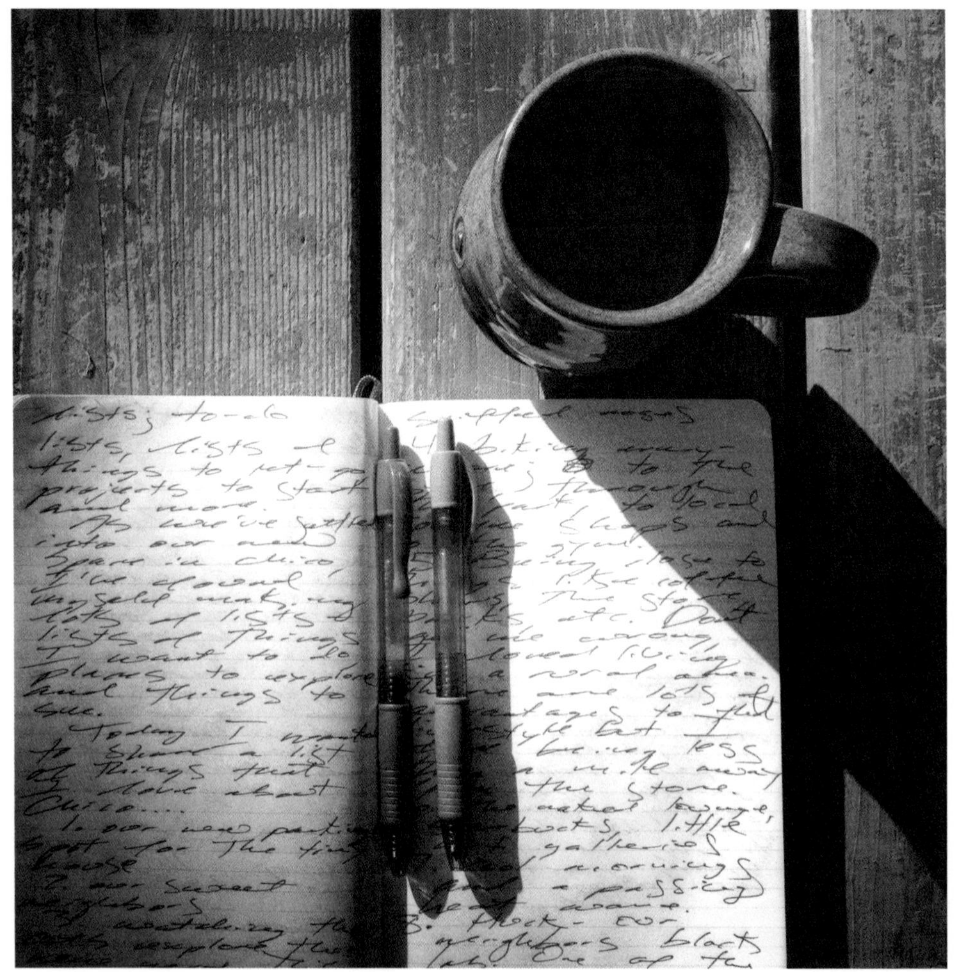

Write to heal.

"By engaging in lament, we care for ourselves.
For not to express grief is to put ourselves at risk for isolation, for illness."

— Louise DeSalvo

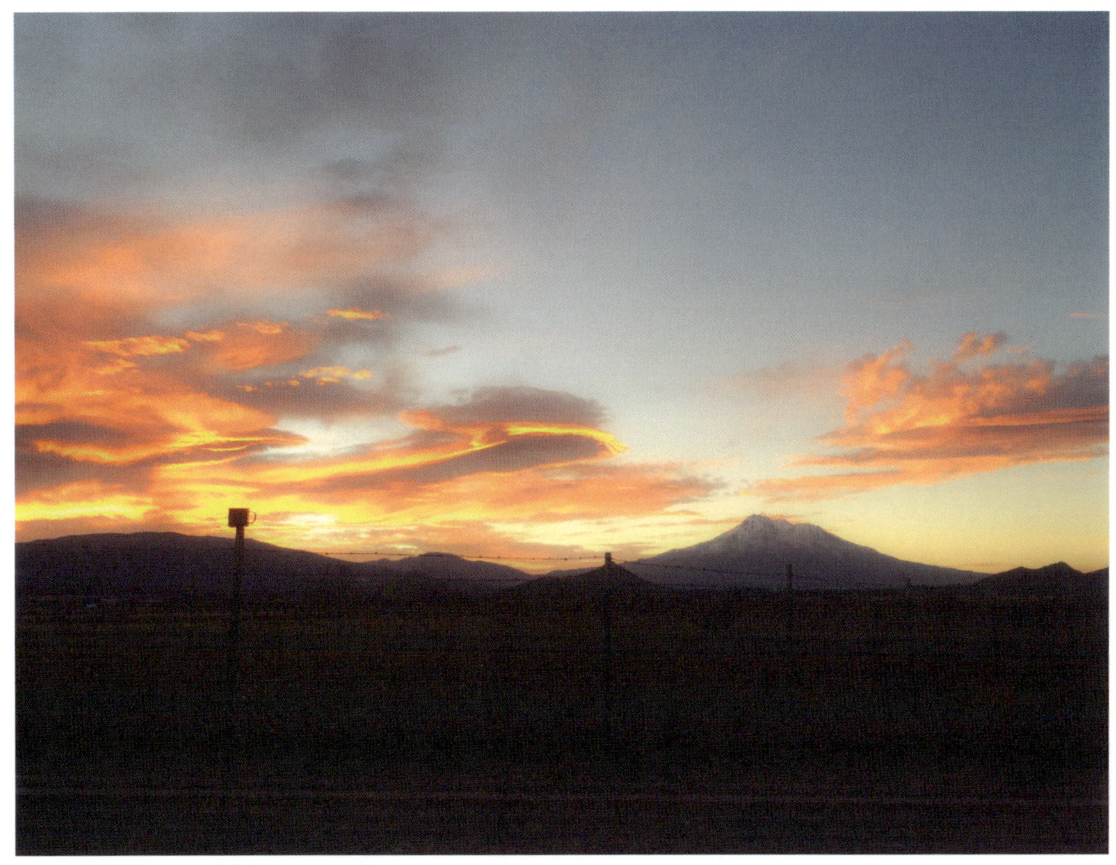

No filter needed.

When I'm sad, all I have to do is walk out my front door, and I'm reminded that nature is amazing. When the sky is on fire, you don't need a fancy camera or editing tools.

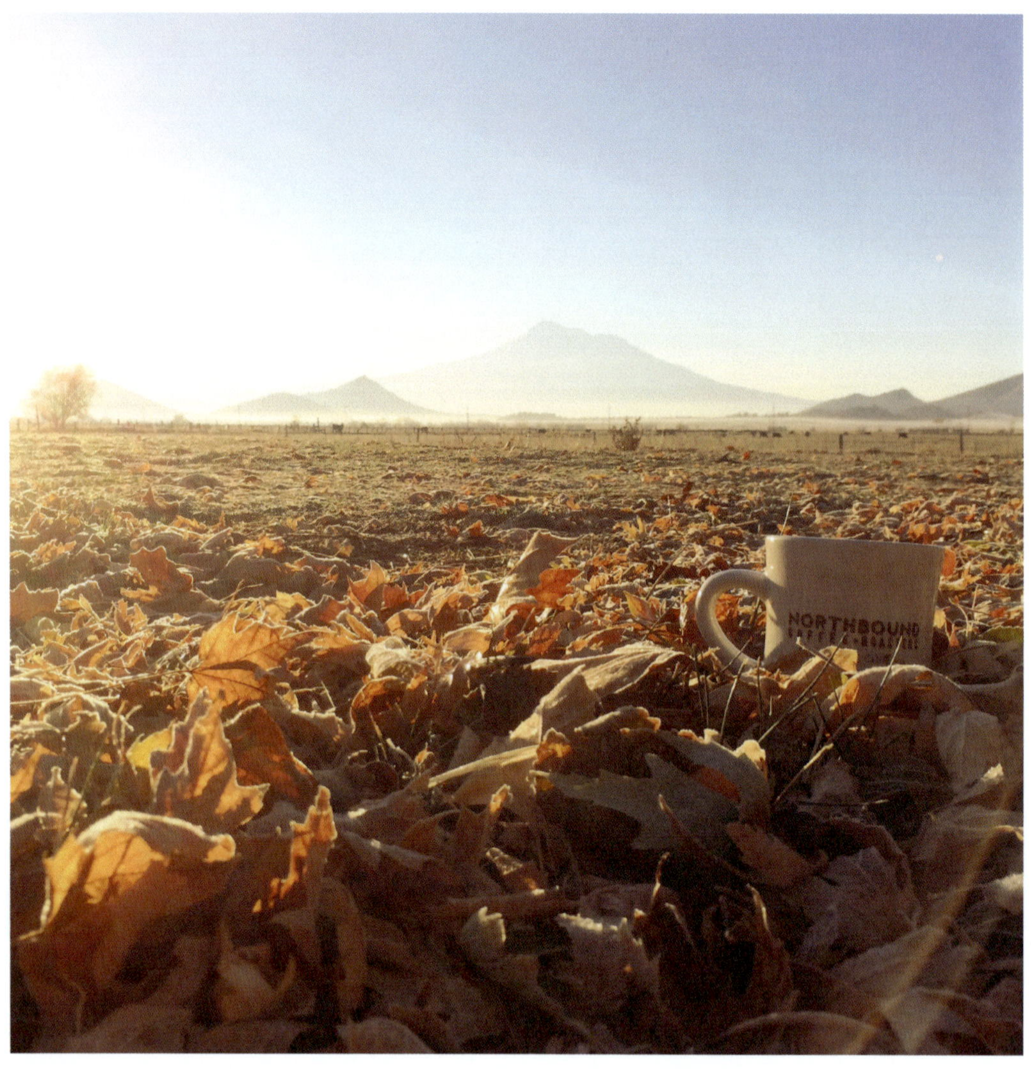

Epic sunrises.

Consider shooting into the sun. Typically, photographers are instructed to not shoot into the light. However, shooting into the light can give you the ability to create stunning silhouettes.

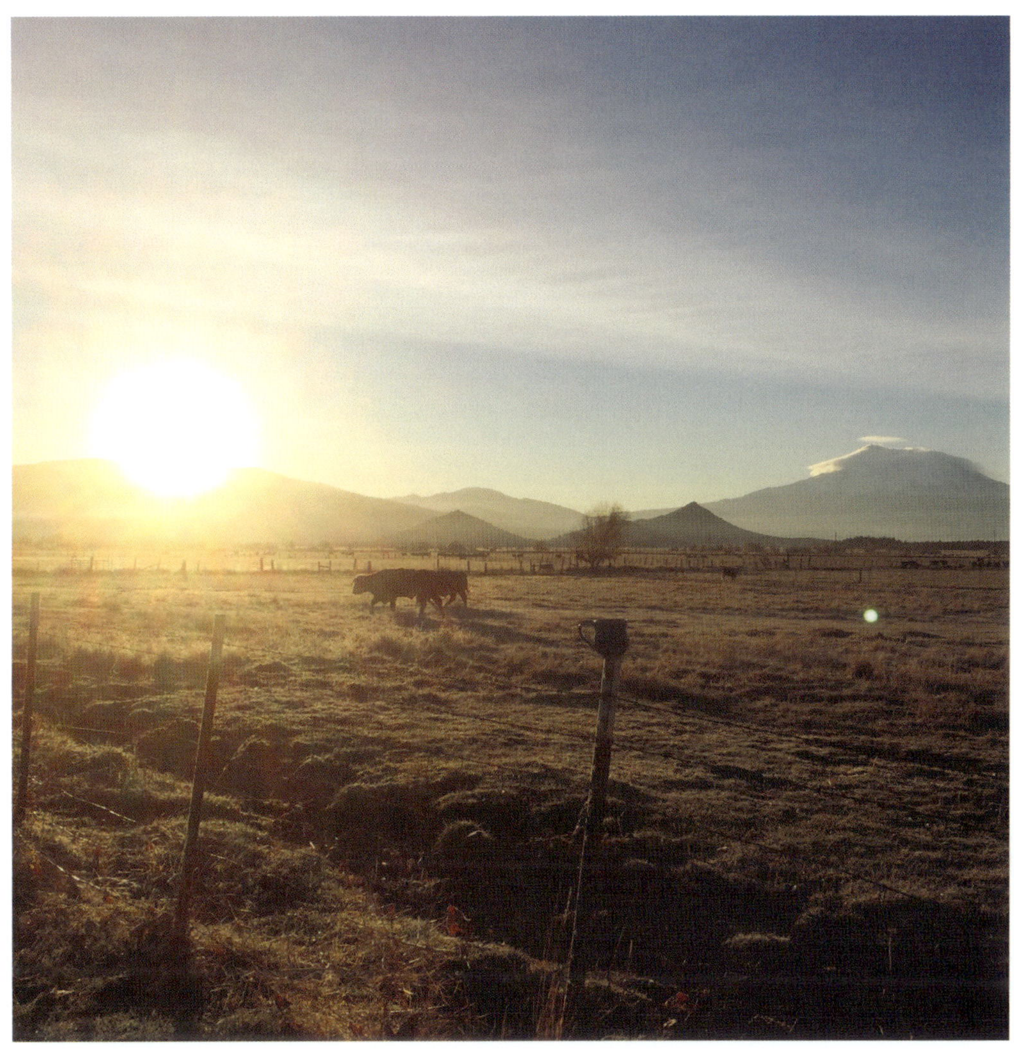

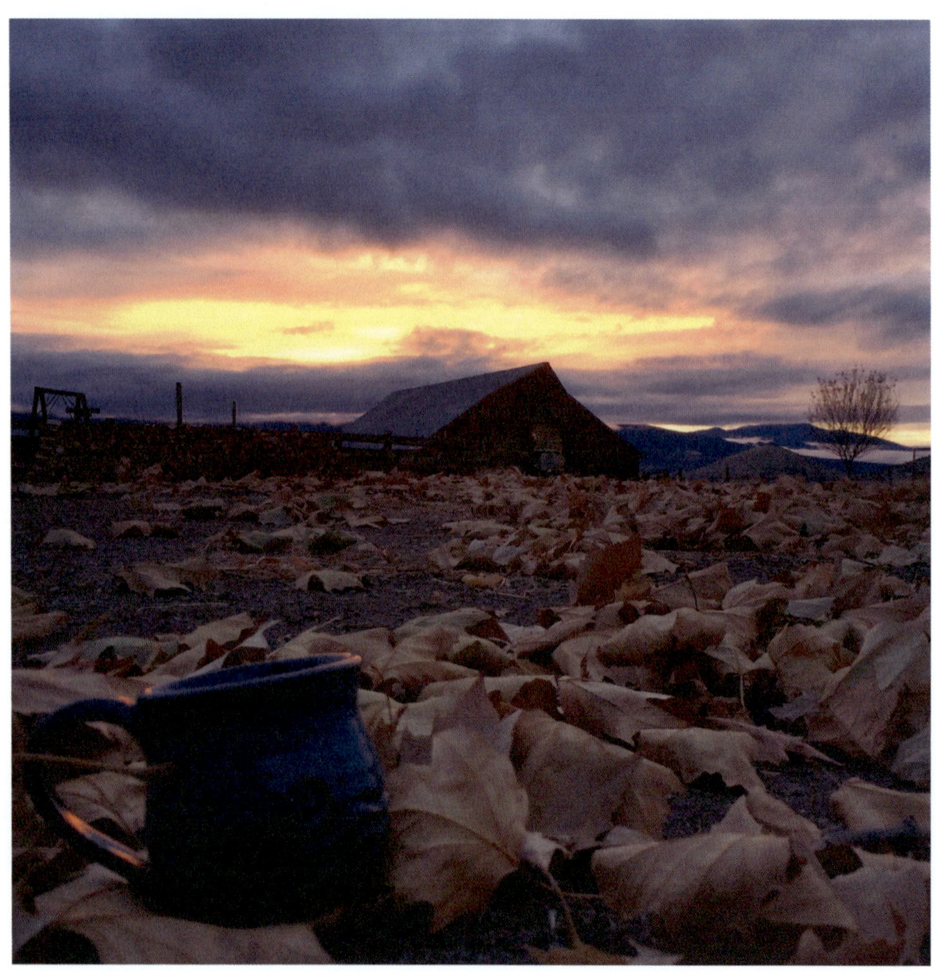

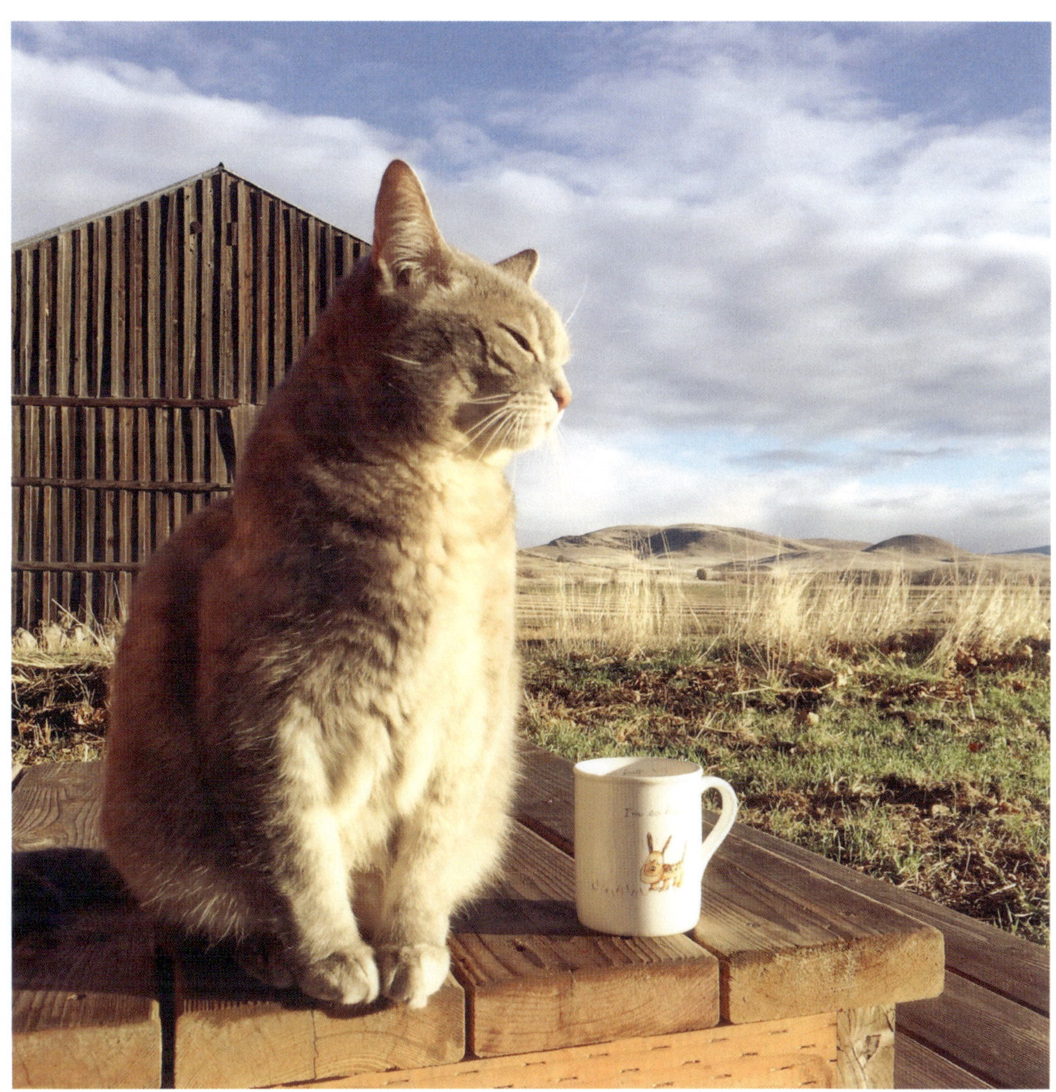

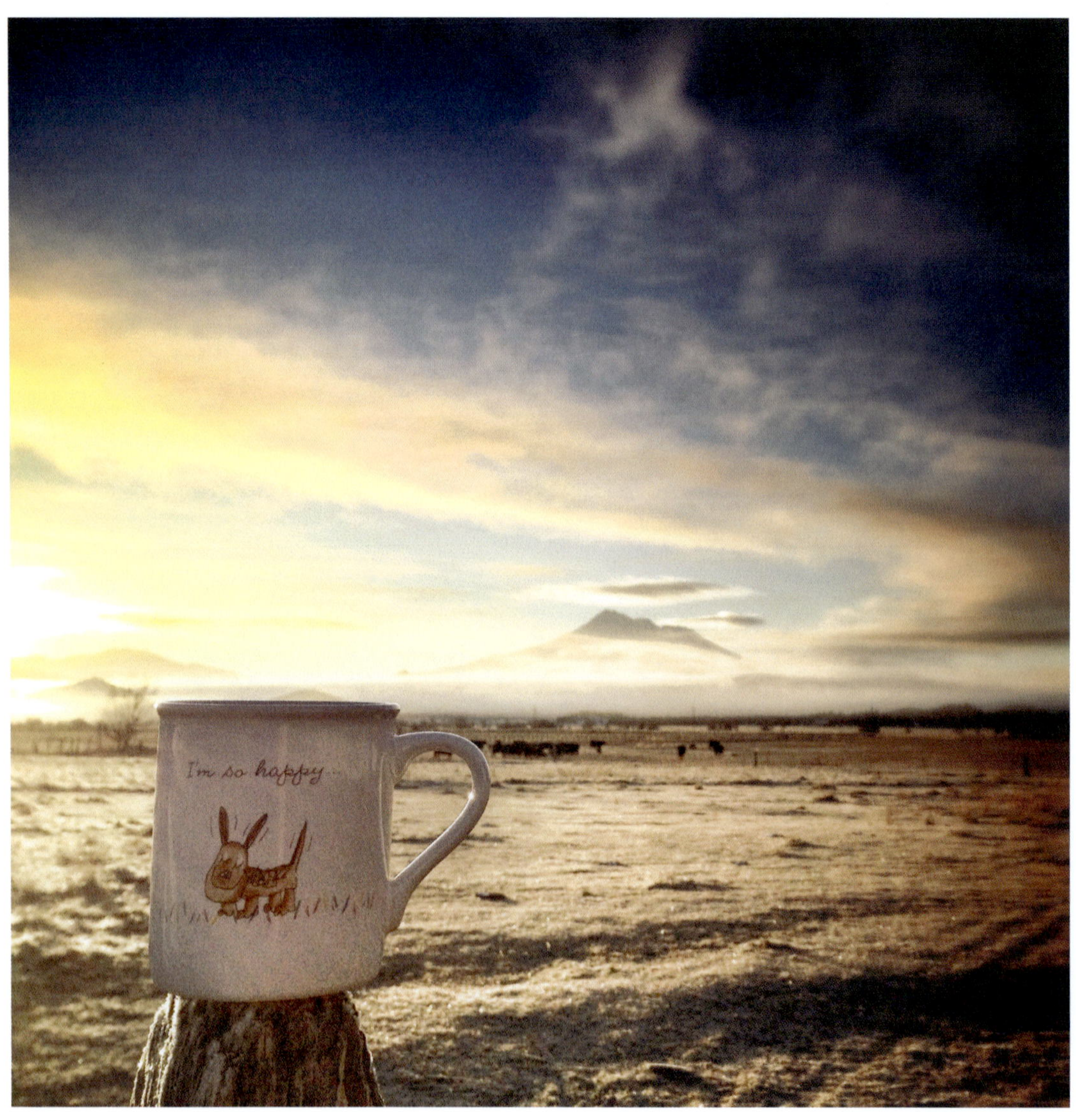
I'm so happy

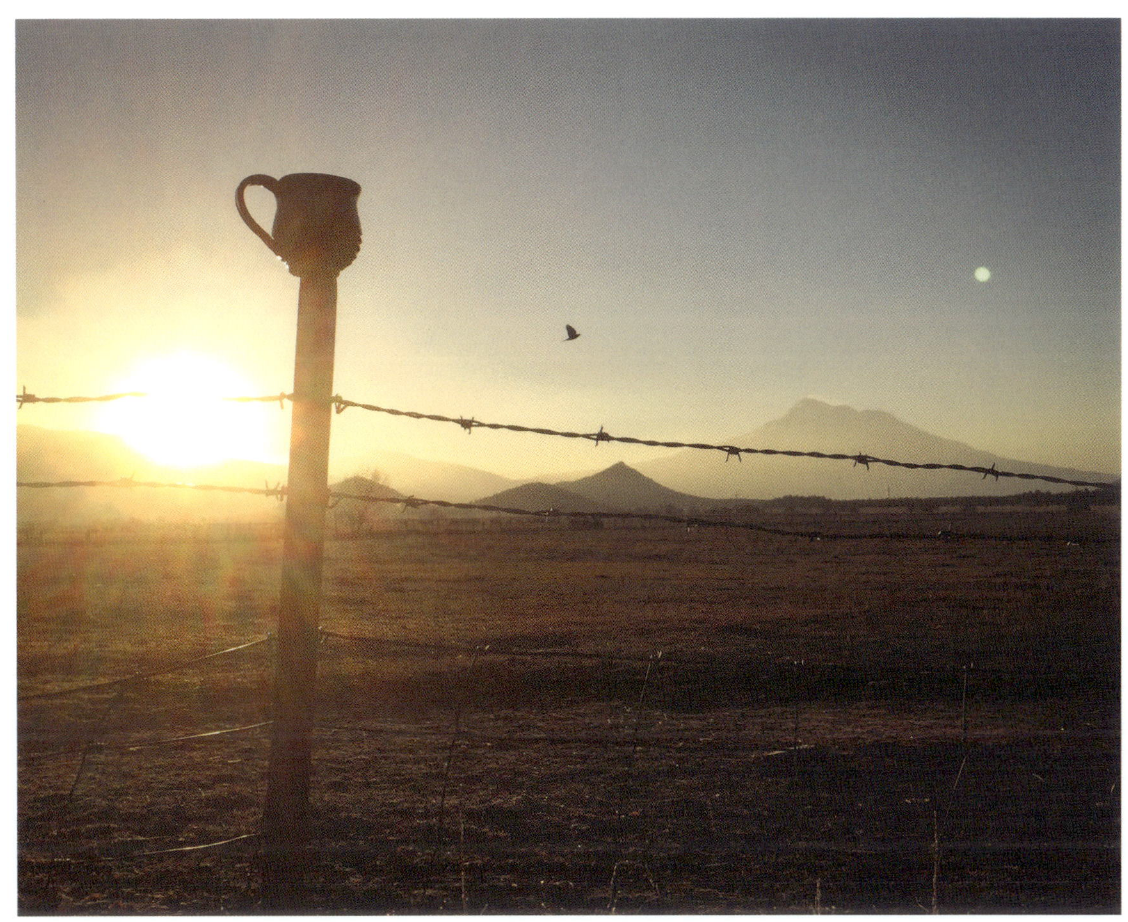

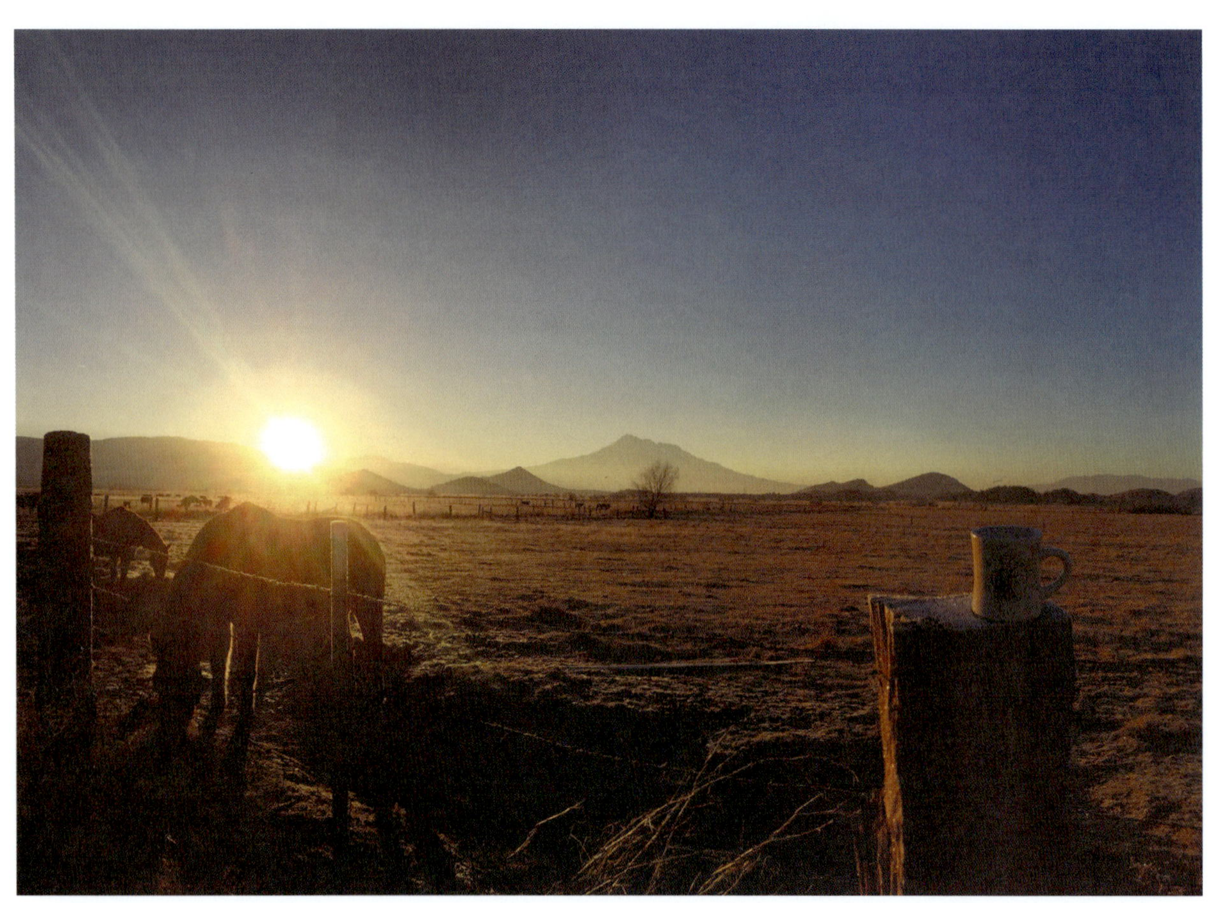

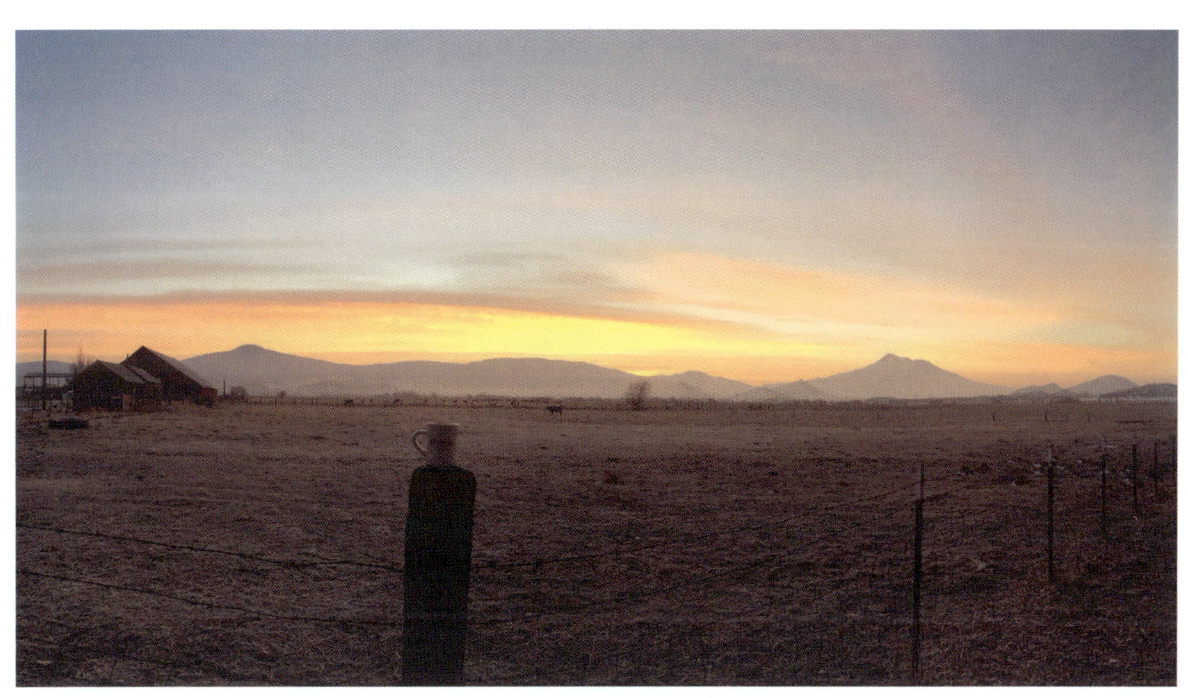

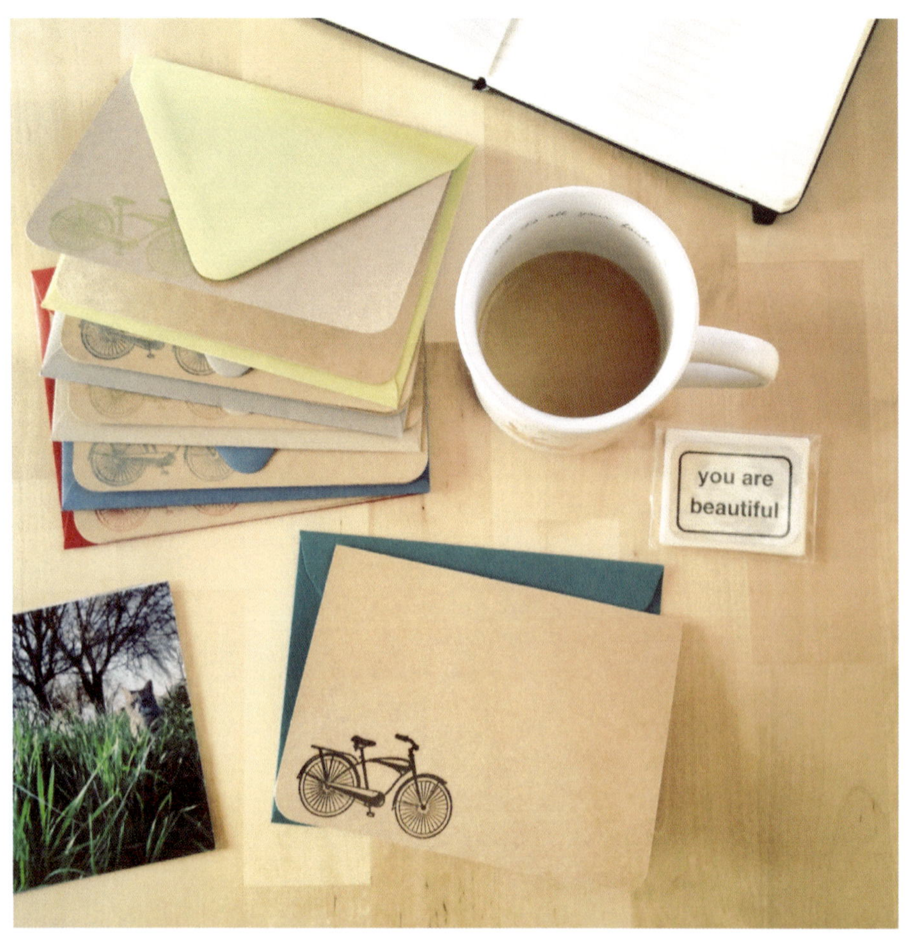

Letters.

"A real love letter is made of insight, understanding, and compassion. Otherwise it's not a love letter. A true love letter can produce a transformation in the other person, and therefore in the world. But before it produces a transformation in the other person, it has to produce a transformation within us. Some letters may take the whole of our lifetime to write."

— Thích Nhất Hạnh

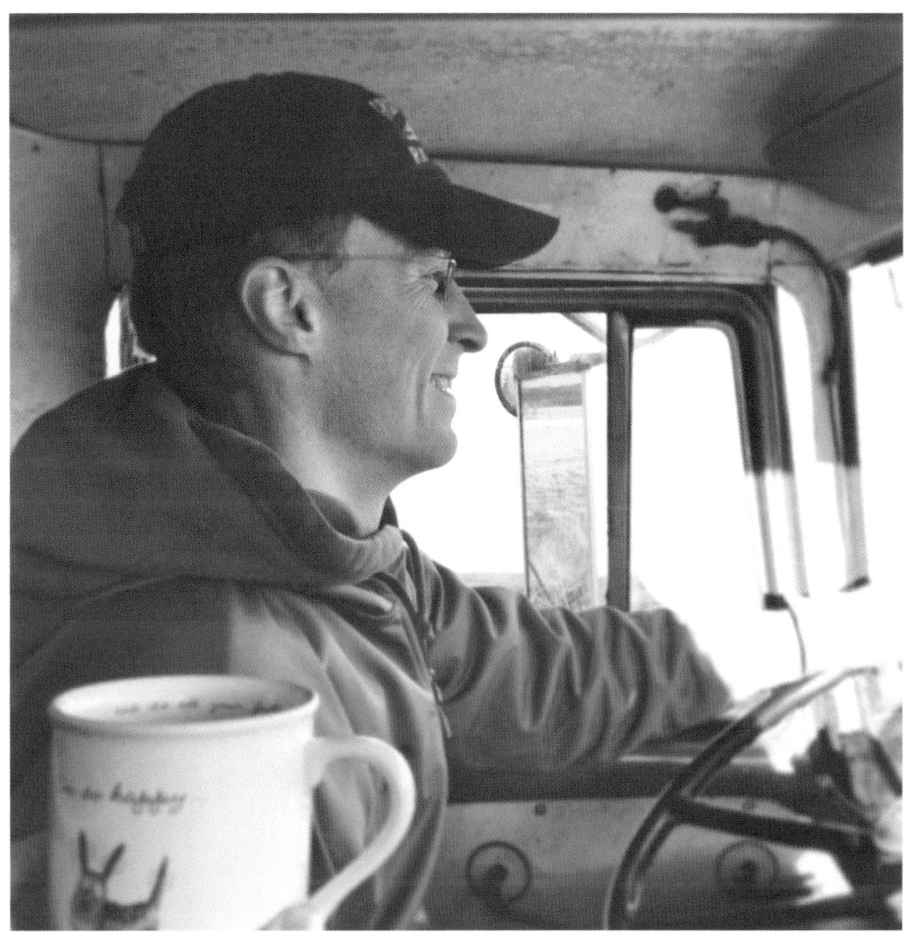

My love.

Meet Logan, my sweet husband and best friend. I snapped this image in early 2013, while Logan was driving a feed truck on the ranch. It was the first time I helped Logan feed the cows. As the passenger, it was my job to hop out and open up gates as we came to them. It was a fun, cold, and frosty morning. I loved how the cows followed the feed truck and gathered around like it was the local coffee house.

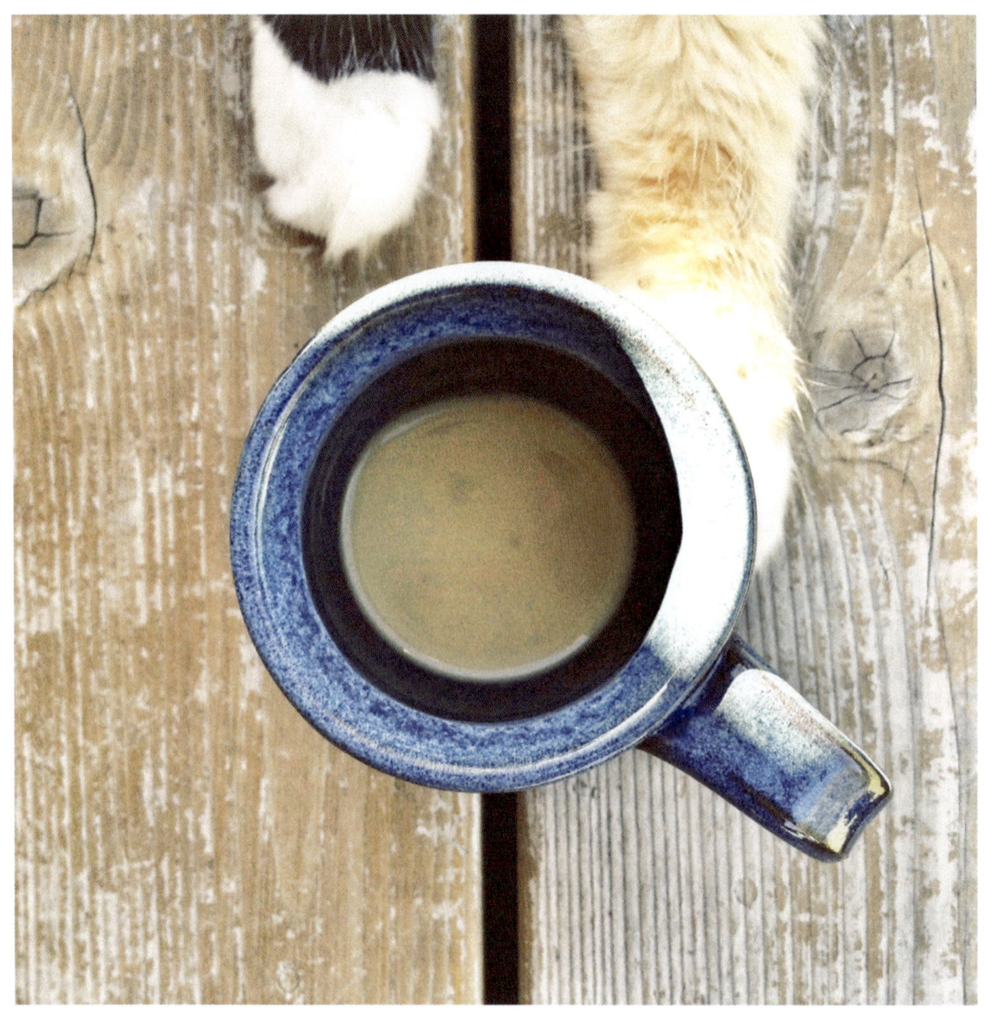

Pawed.

I sat down on our porch next to my cat, Christie, in June 2013. It was already 70 degrees outside, and it was only 7:00 a.m.! I was ready to write in my journal, and I set my coffee cup down next to Christie. When I looked over, I saw that her paw was resting gently on my cup!

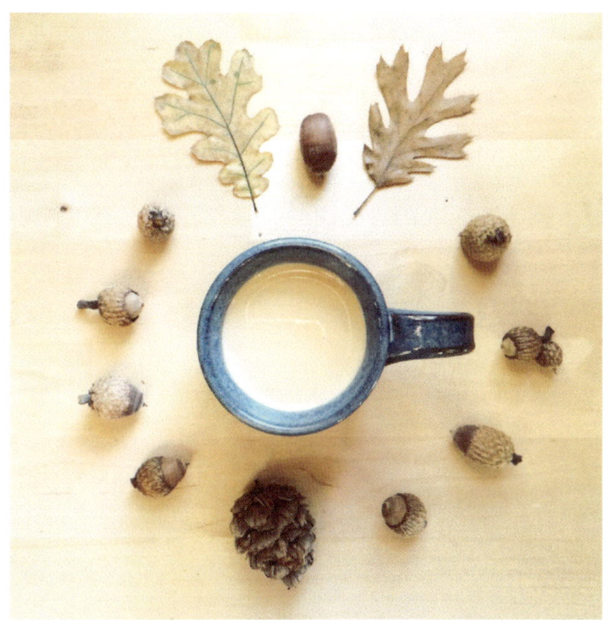

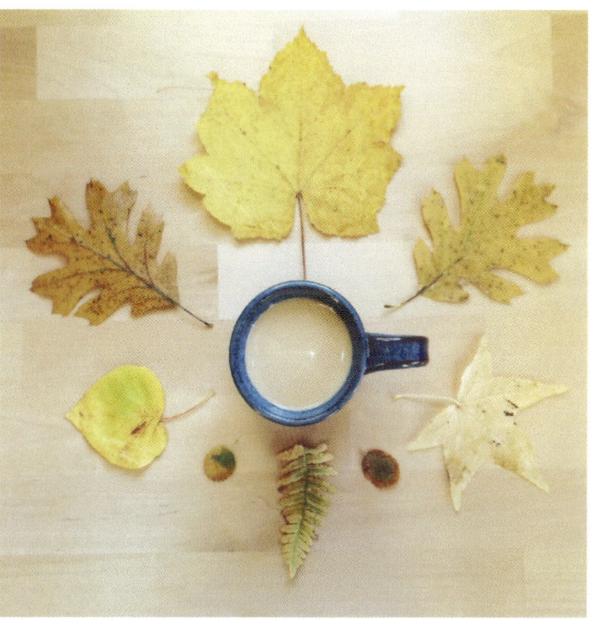

Fall collections.

On November 16, 2013, Mahlon would have turned 71 years old. When Mahlon was healthy, he loved going on long, weekend hikes with his friends. To celebrate Mahlon's birthday and life, Logan and I hiked the Castle Crag trail. It was an eight-mile round-trip hike that led to stunning views of the Crags, Castle Dome, and Mt. Shasta. Mahlon would have loved it! On the hike, I collected leaves, acorns, and pine cones. I used the goodies for a few morning view photographs.

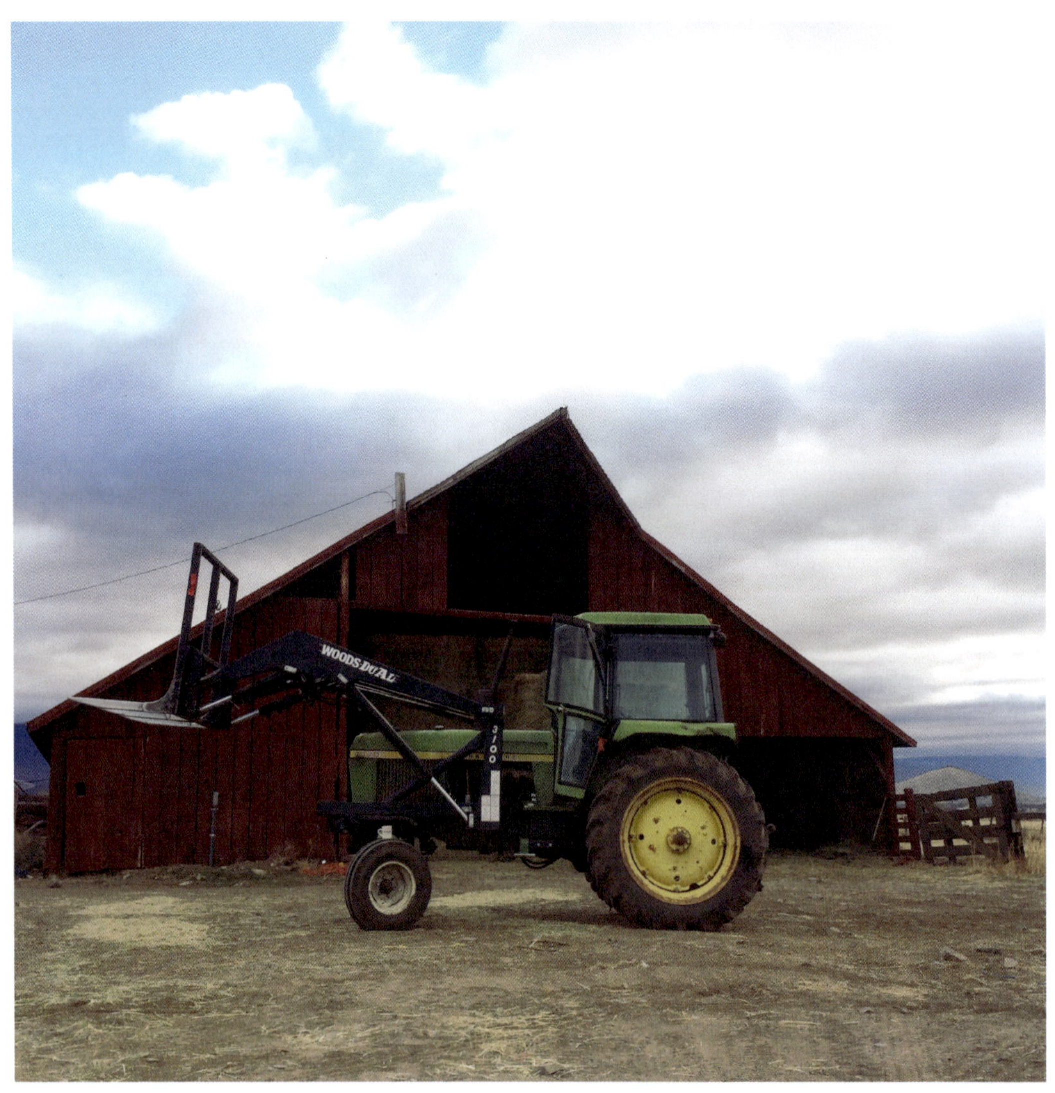

Lost coffee cups.

Don't let low-light situations deter you from snapping photos. You can always use image-processing software to adjust the exposure, contrast, and highlights in the image.

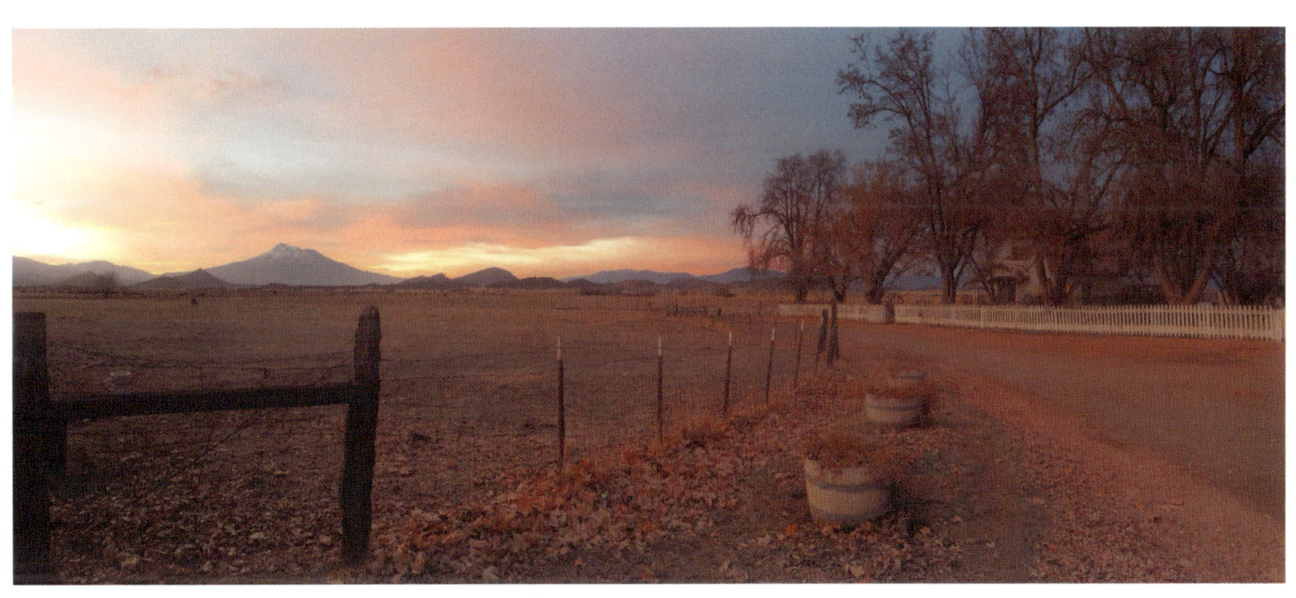

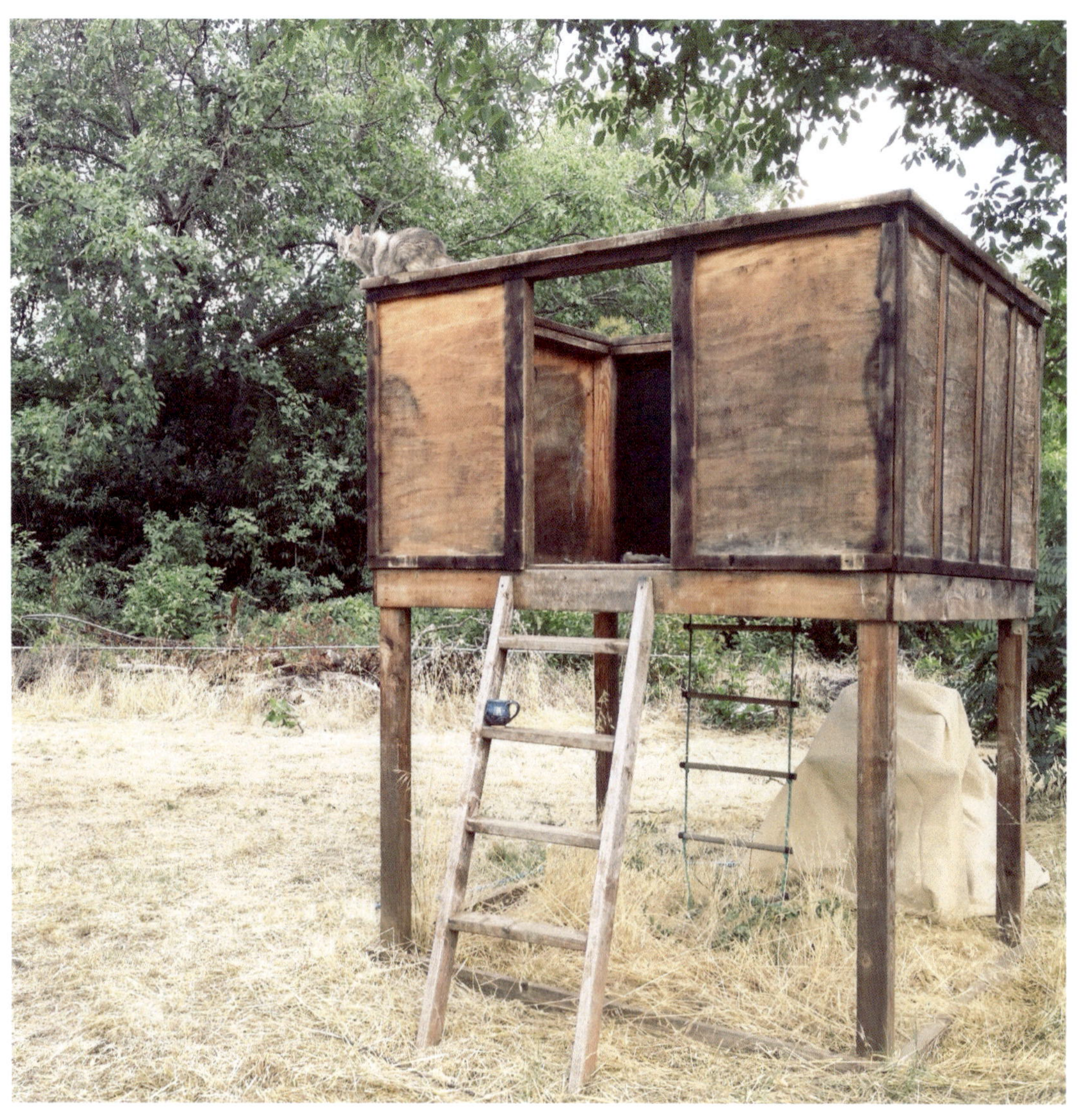

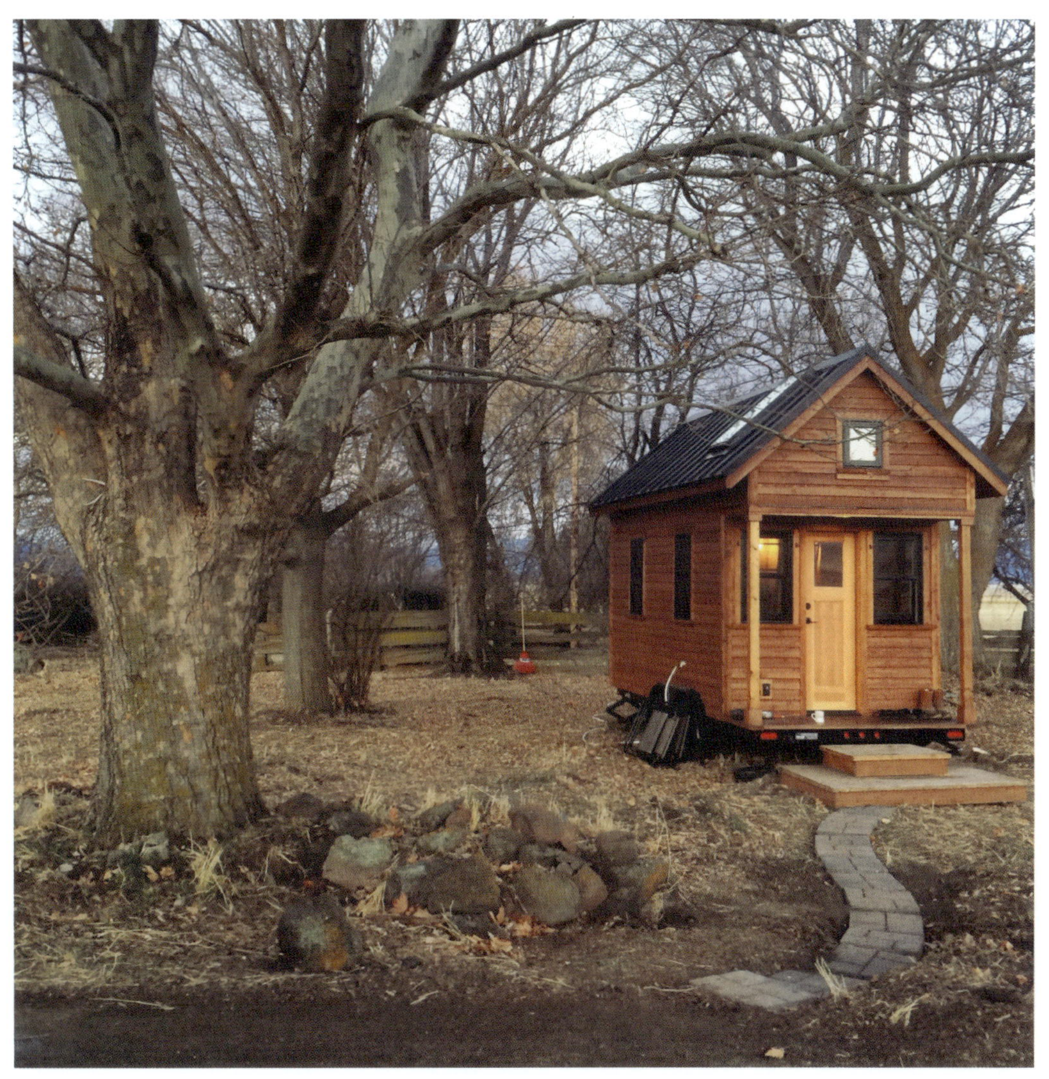

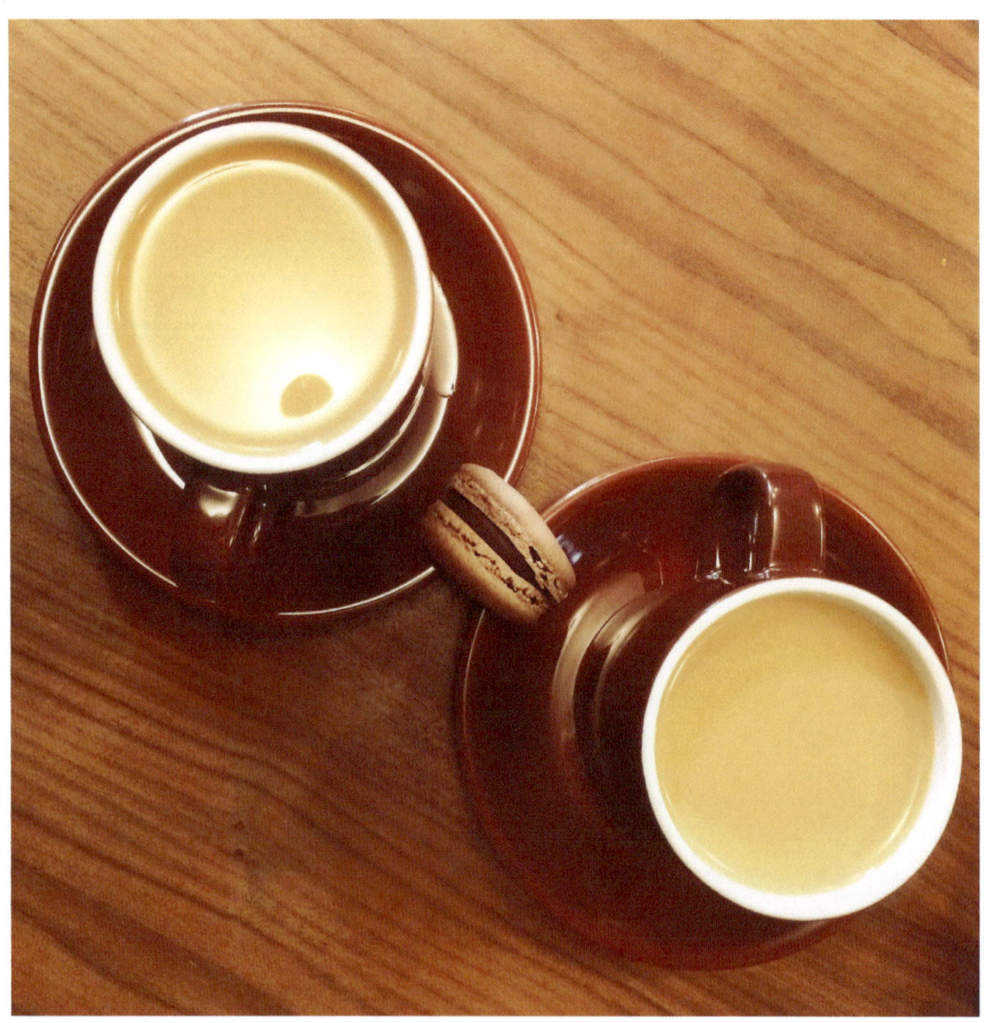

Ashland.

We spent hours walking around Ashland, Oregon, on November 6, 2013—my thirty-fifth birthday. It was fun to explore residential areas, downtown, and Lithia Park. I wished Mahlon could have seen the stunning fall colors and had a cup of coffee with us at Mix Sweet Shop.

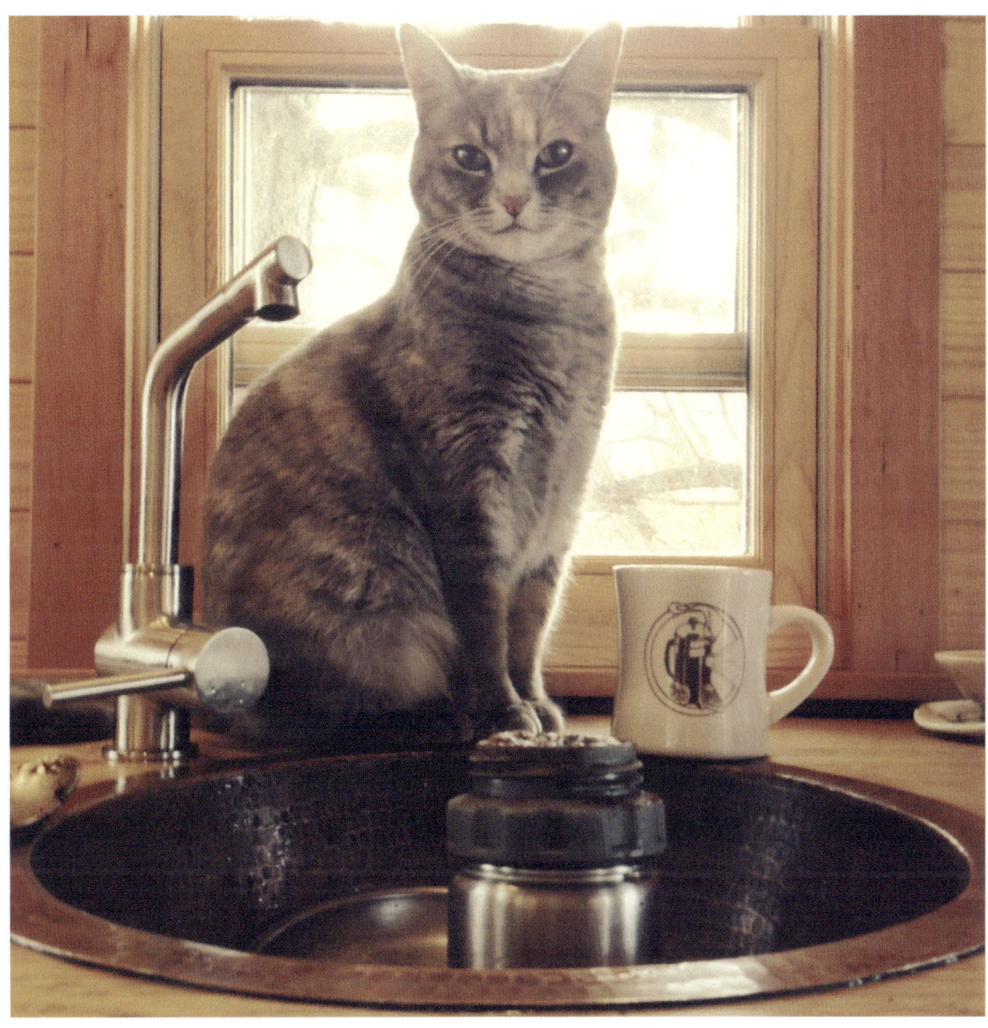

A cute barista.

Elaina, one of my cats, has a bad habit of sitting on the counter in the morning. She loves to help make coffee, and I think she's a cute barista.

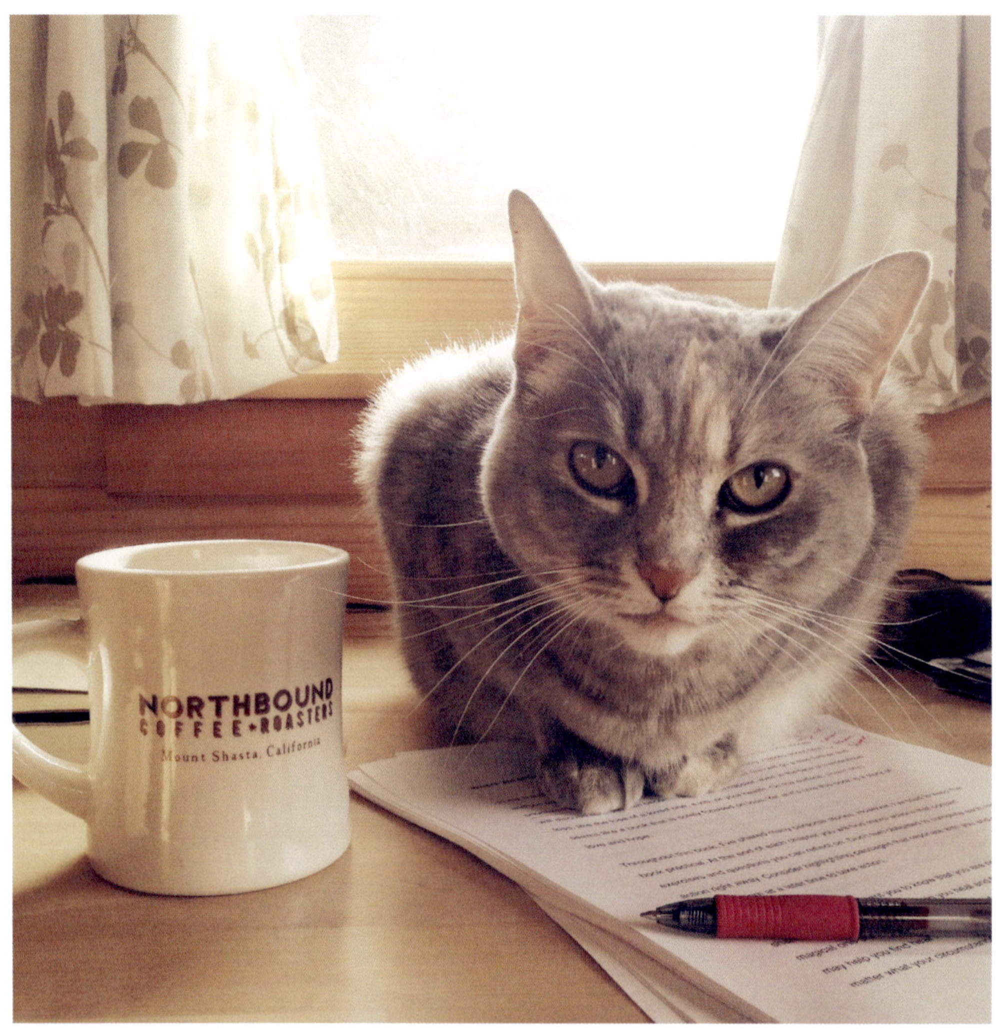

Editorial assistant.

In addition to Elaina's coffee-making duties, she loves providing valuable feedback on my writing projects.

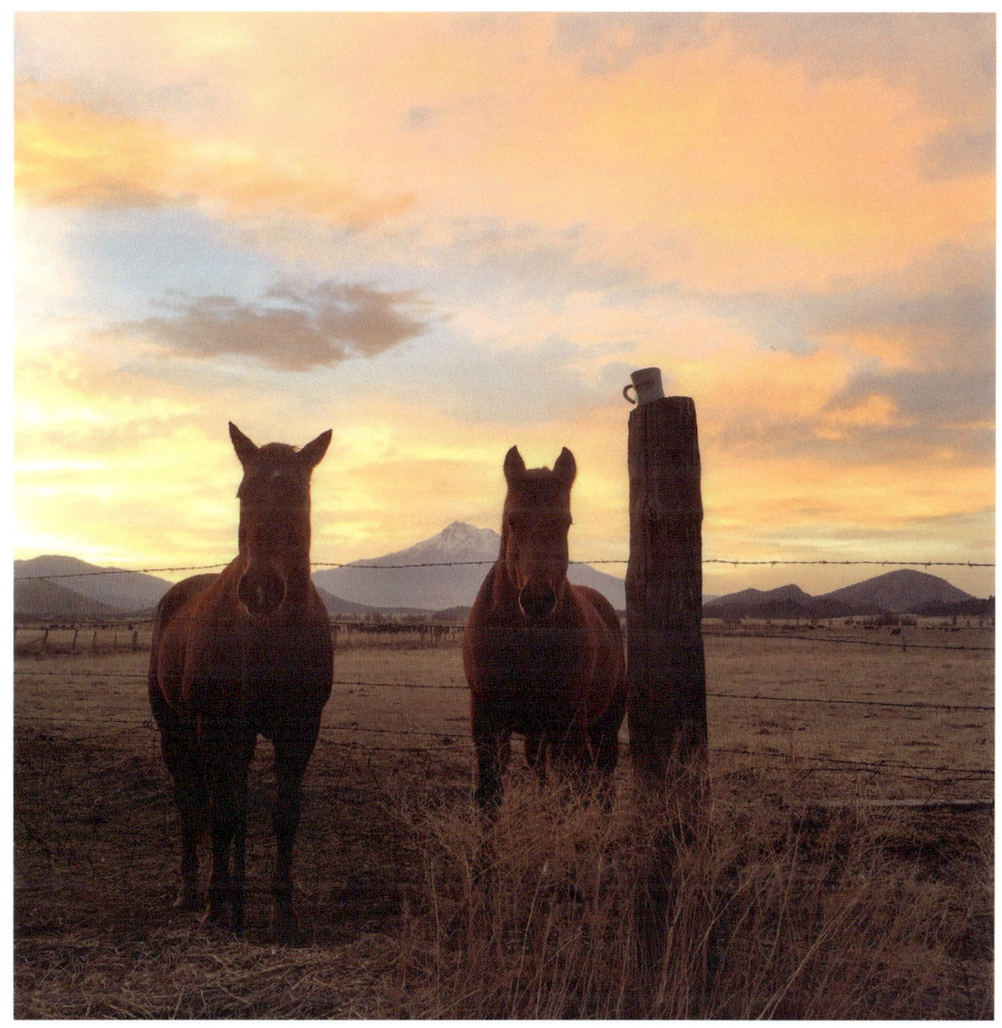

Earl & Smoke.

These two patiently waited for their breakfast while I snapped twenty photos of their cute faces along with the magical sunrise.

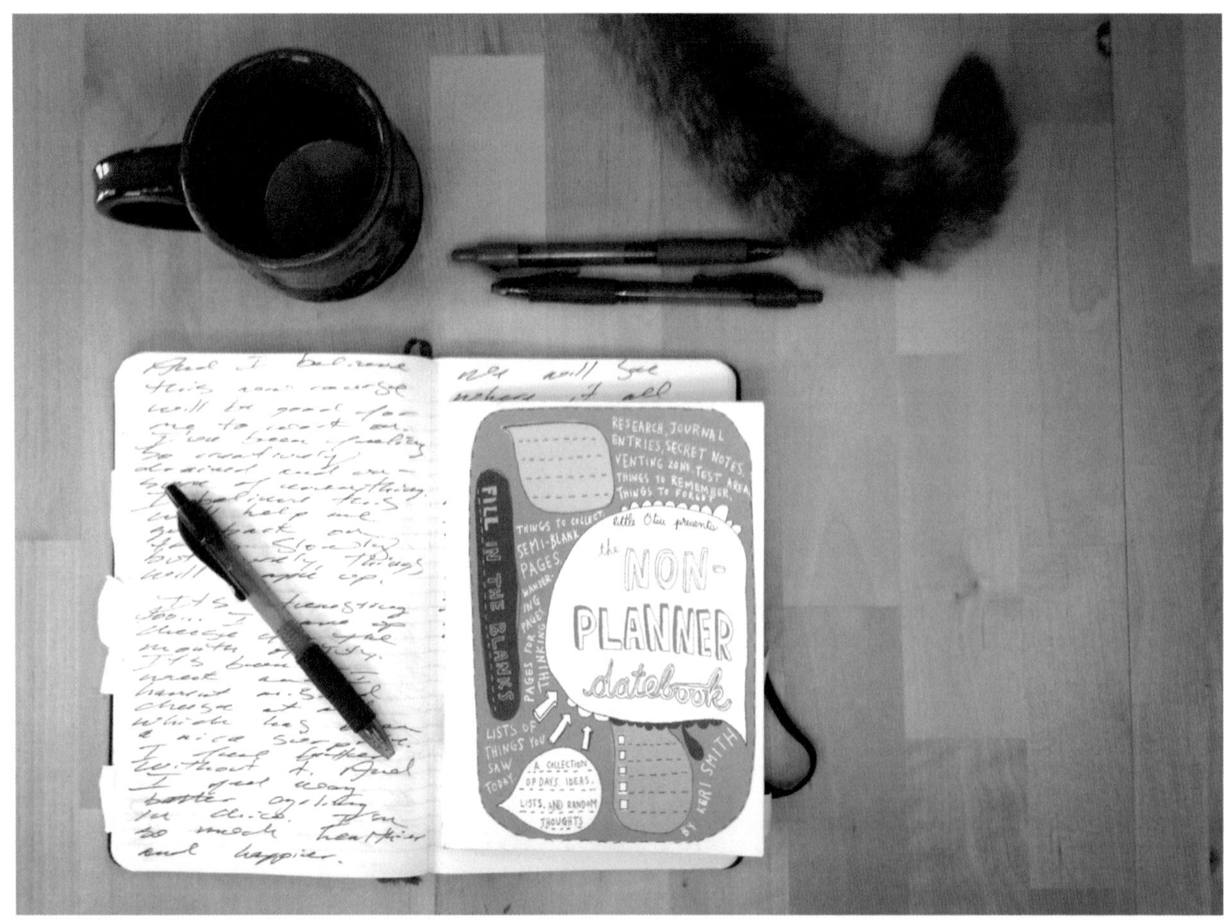

Kitty photo bomb.

When I least expect it, Elaina or Christie make appearances in my shots. Inevitably, they run into the frame or swish their tail as I take the shot. Most of the time, these crazy antics make the image more interesting. And more importantly, they make me laugh.

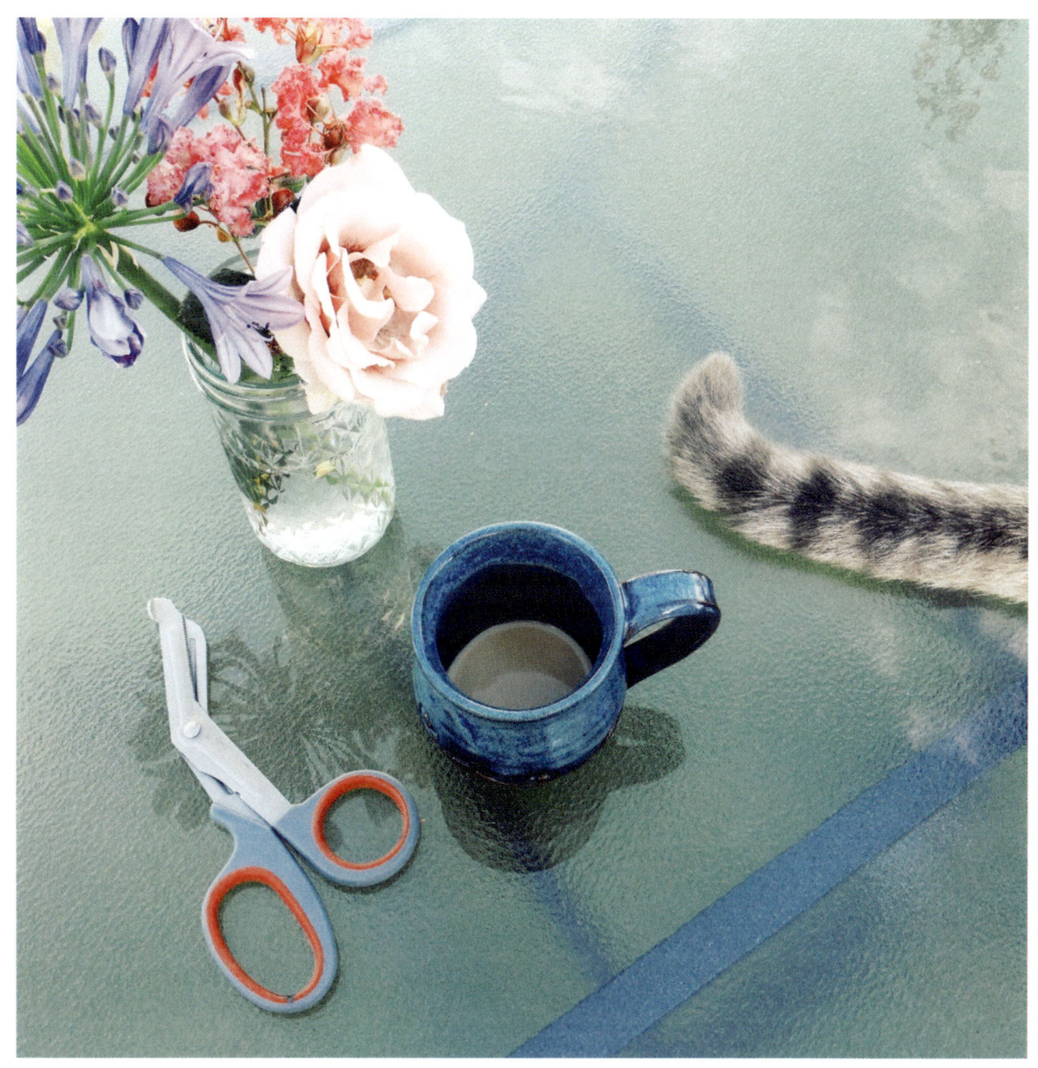

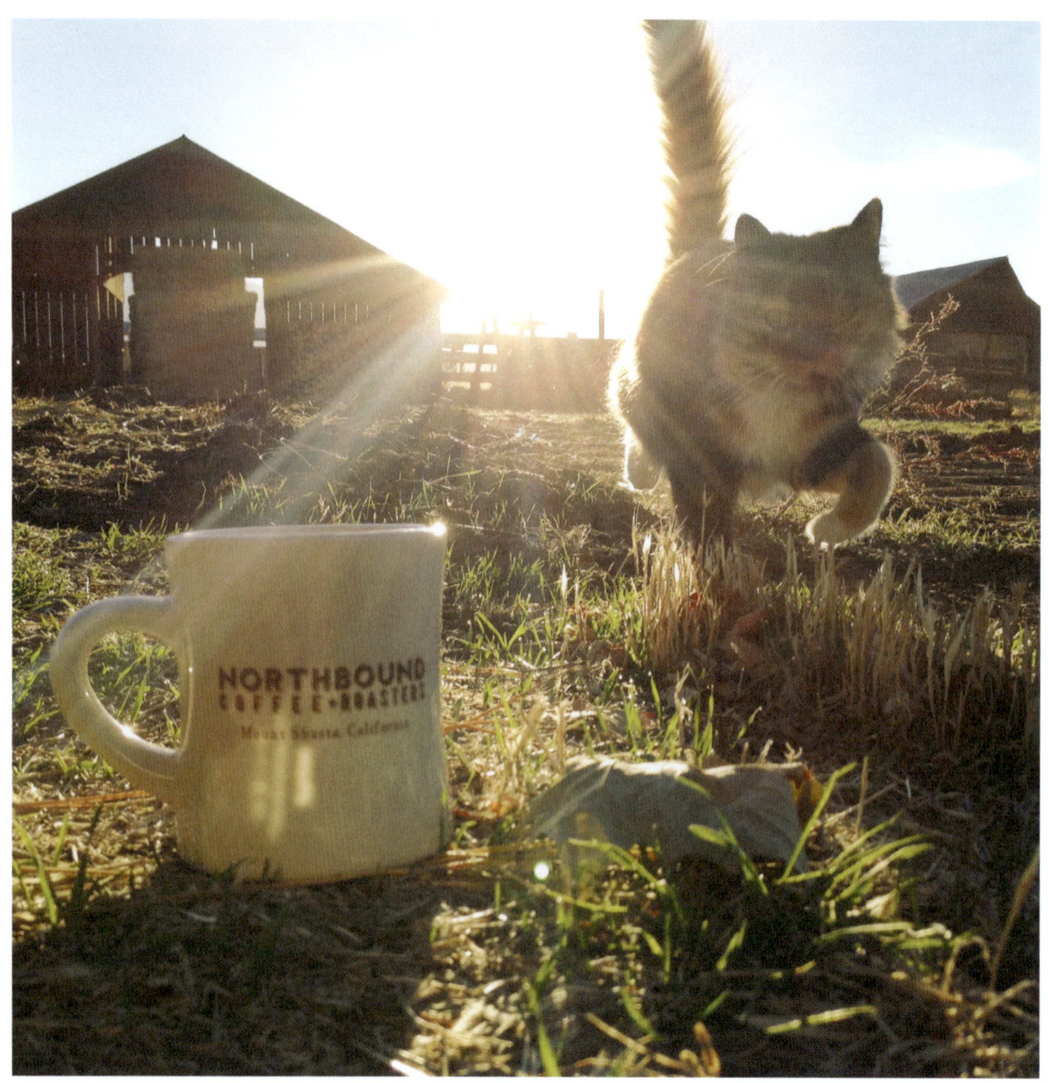
NORTHBOUND

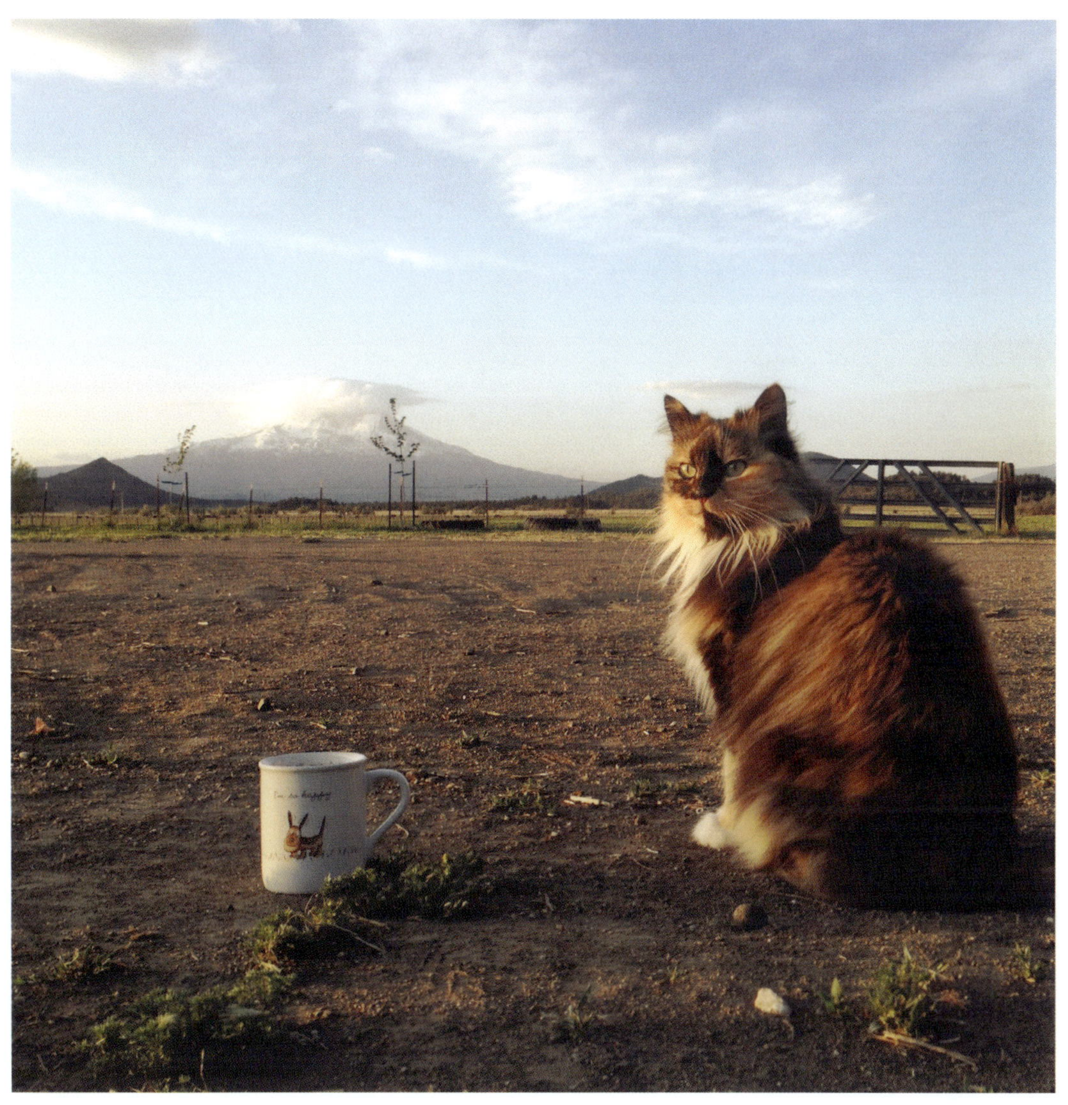

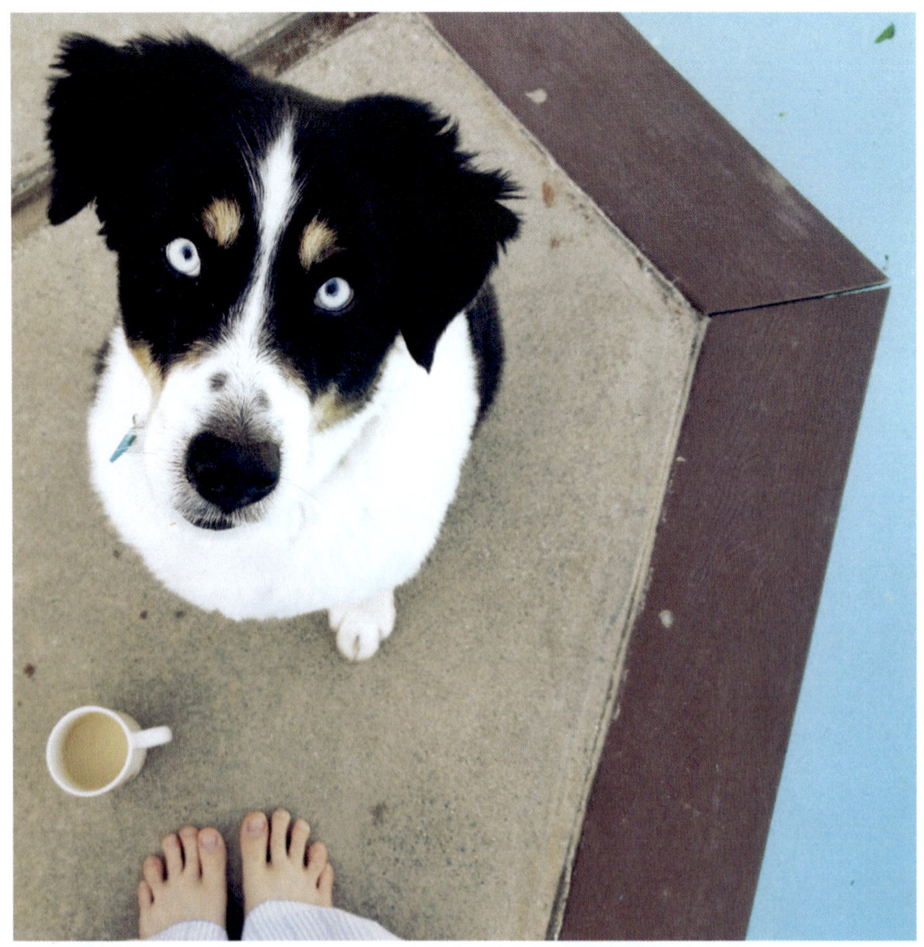

The many faces of Henry.

Henry is a rambunctious Australian shepherd who is my mom's constant companion. He will do anything for a treat, and he has been known to commit various doggy crimes, including counter-surfing for cookies along with eating socks, pillows, sheets, towels, and paper from the garbage can. Henry is also fond of chasing cats and dogs and peeing on my husband's shoe and the pool guy's leg. Mahlon loved this crazy dog, and I do too.

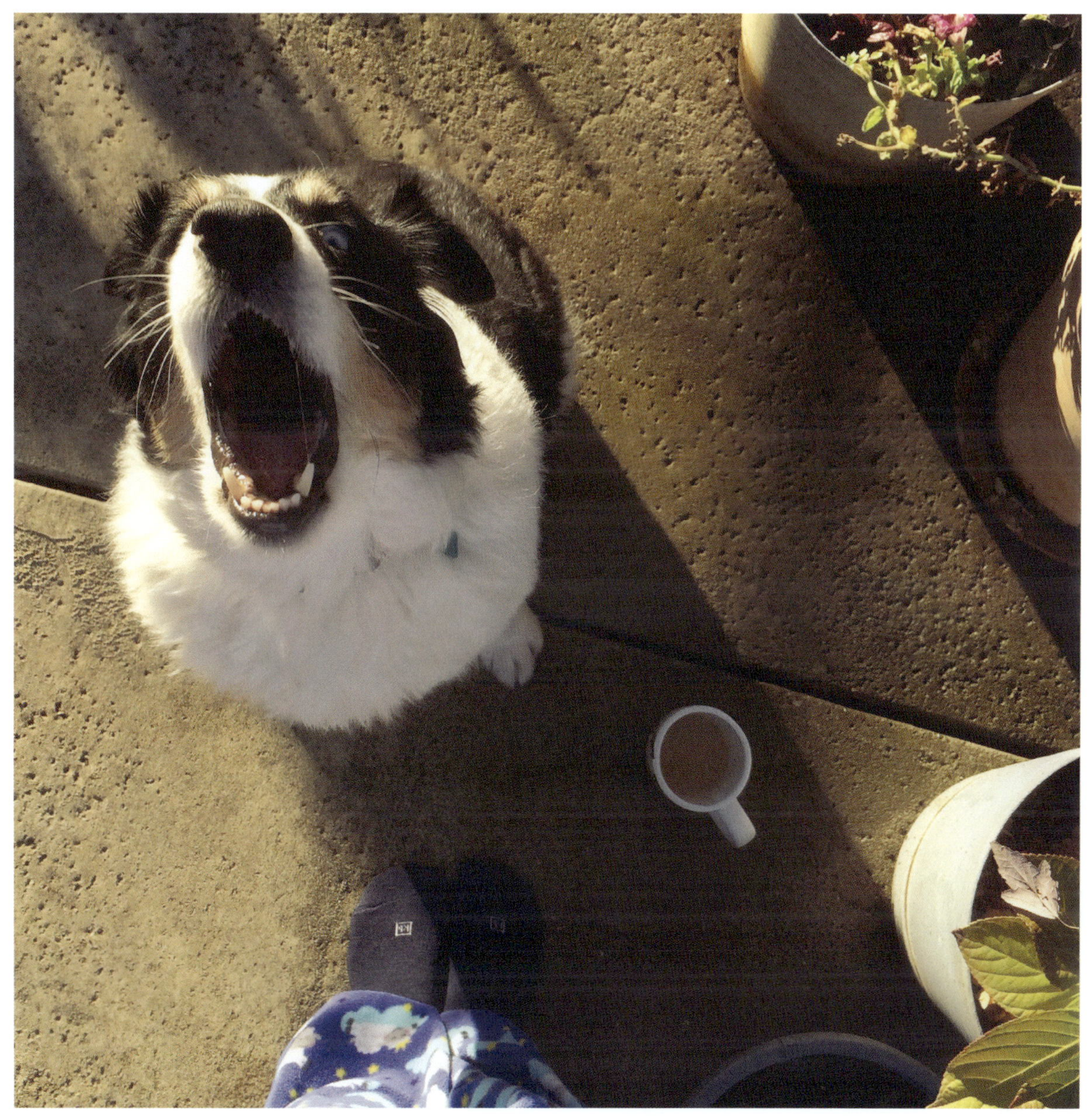

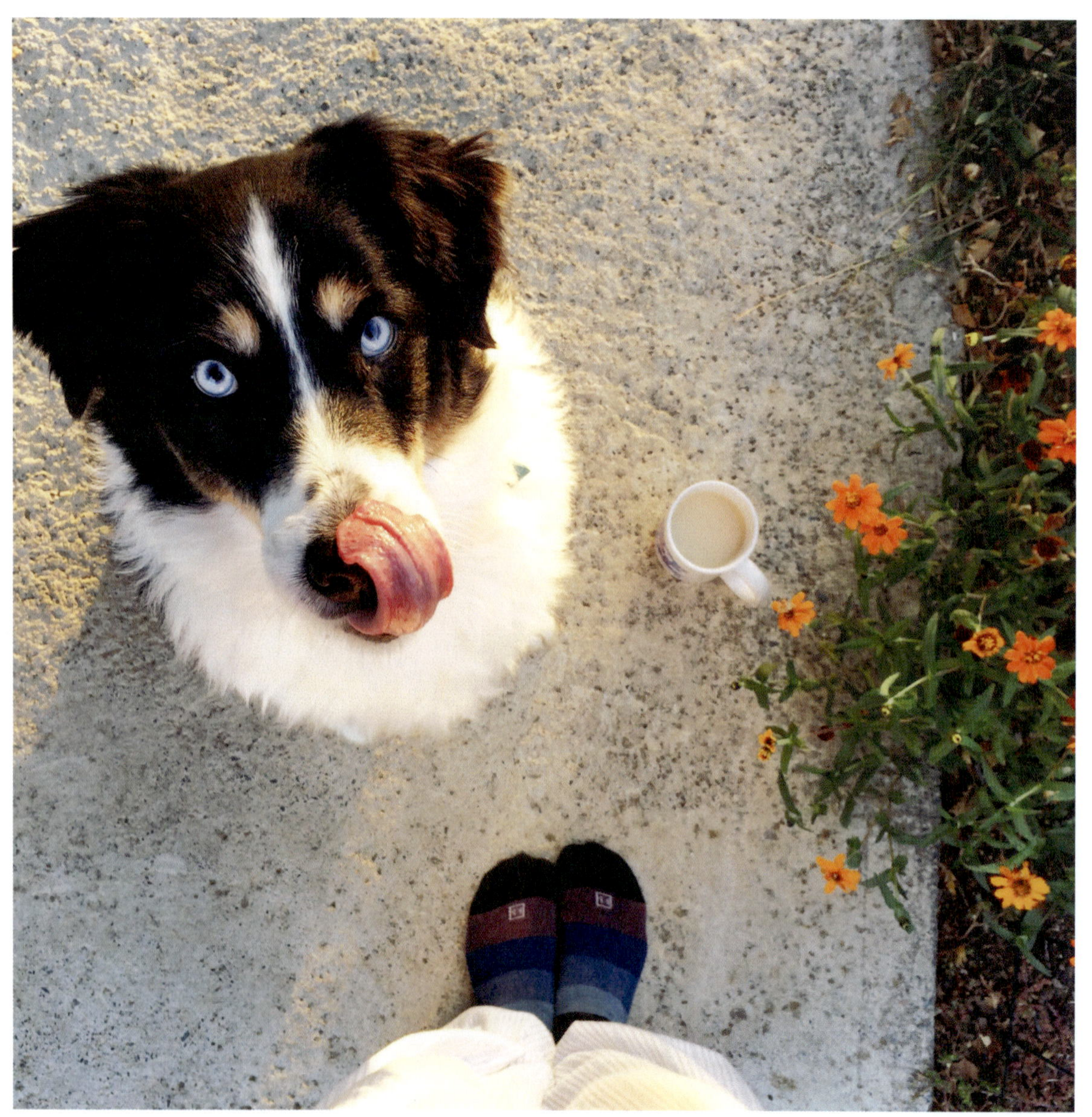

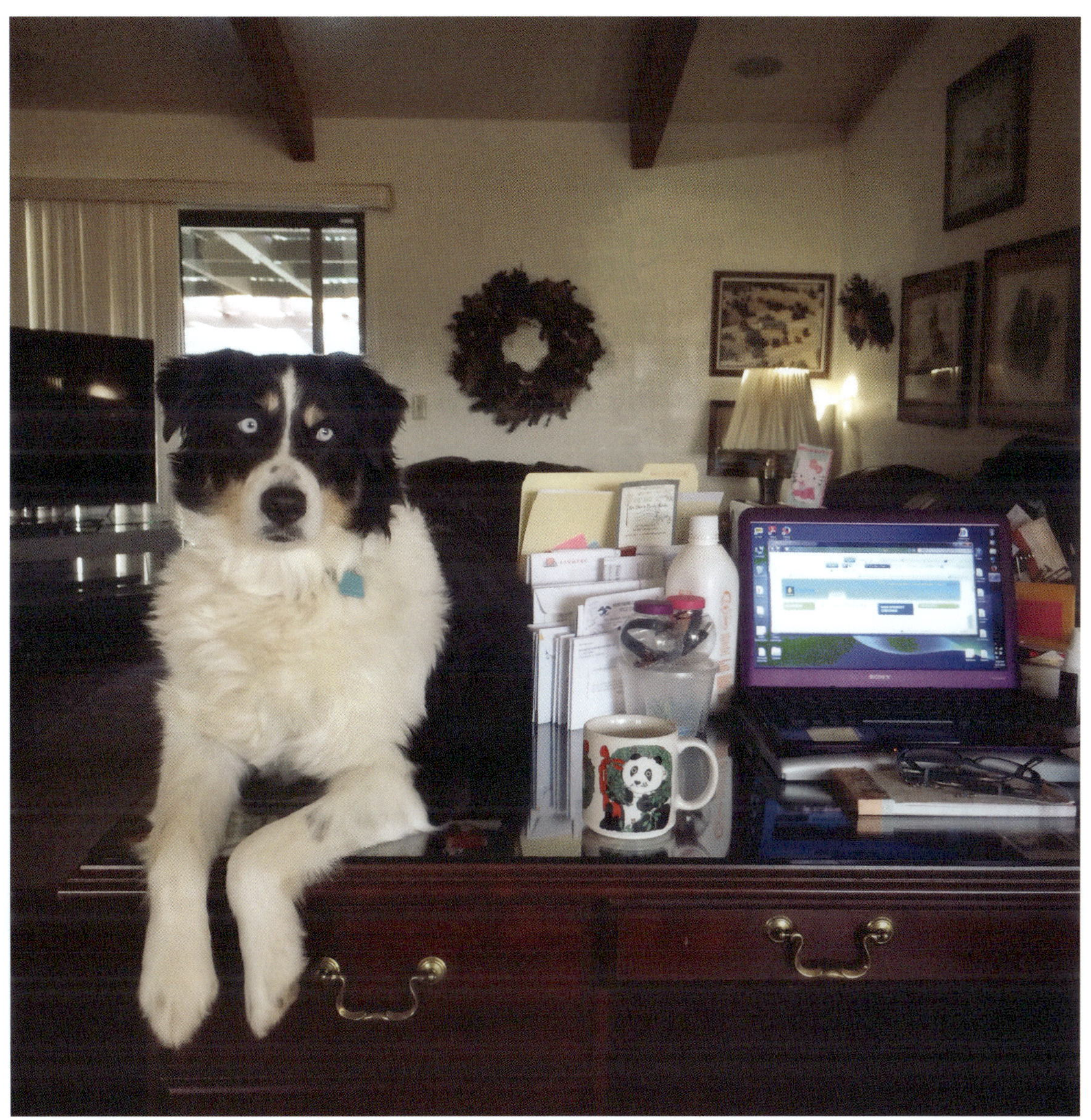

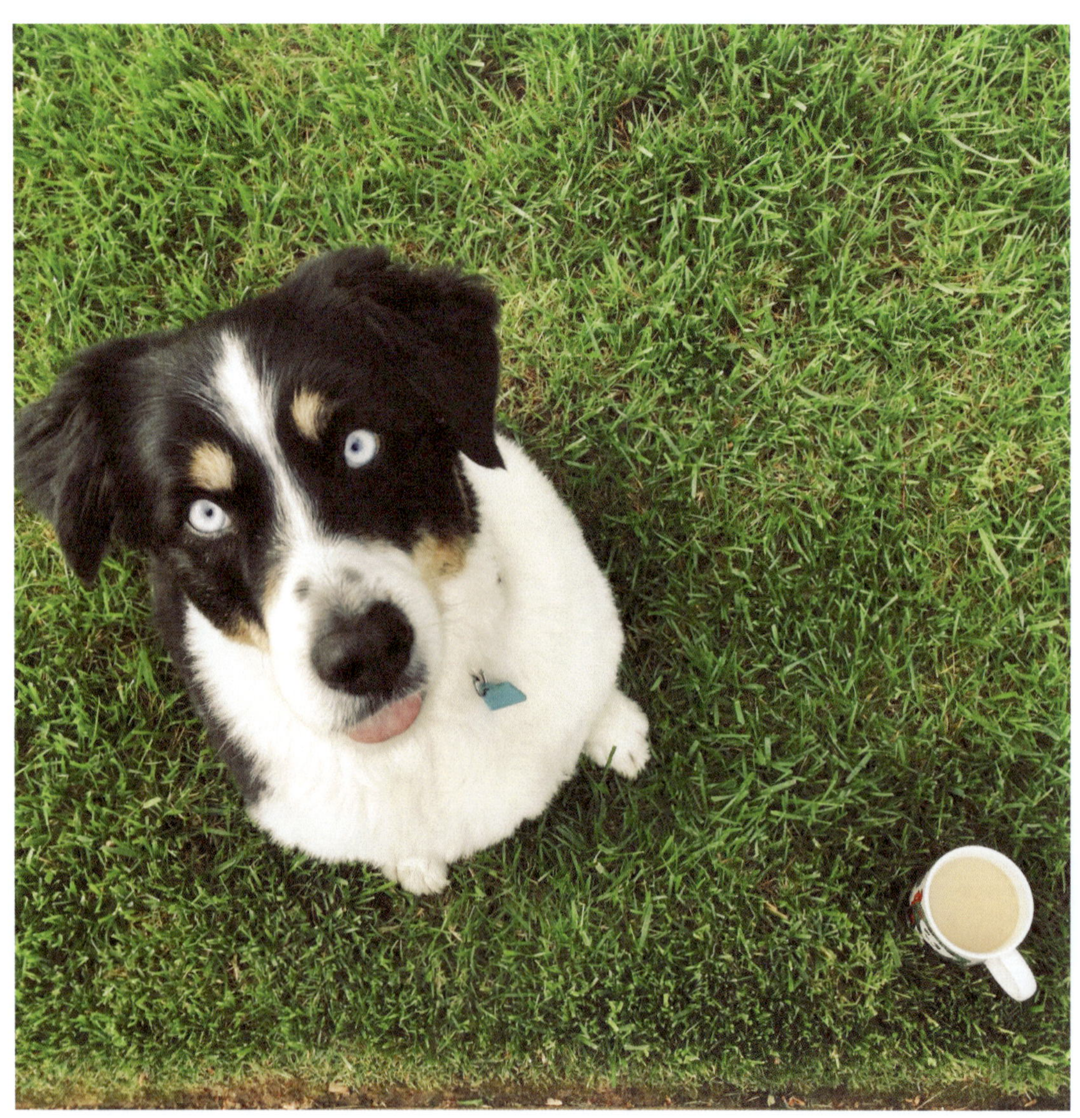

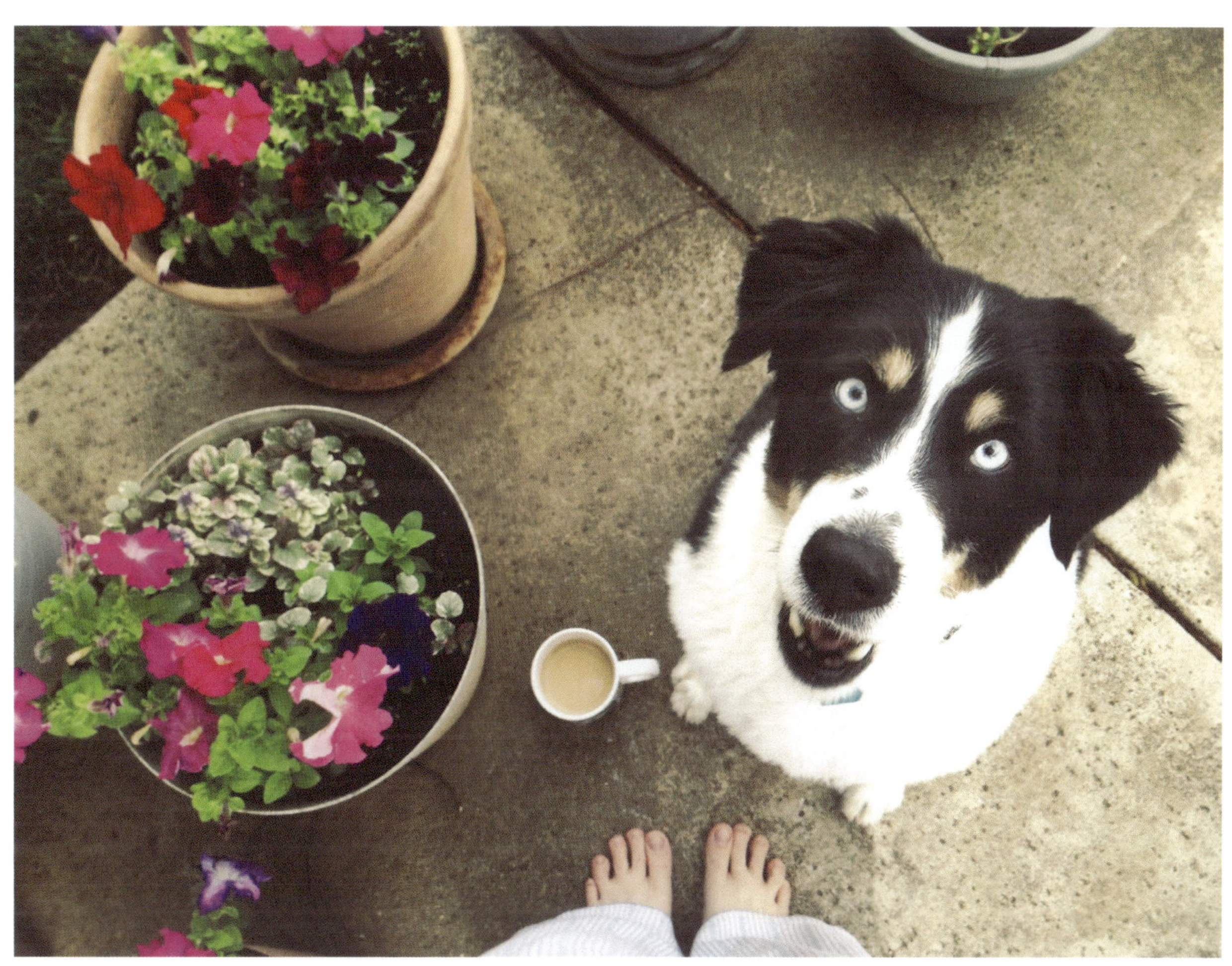

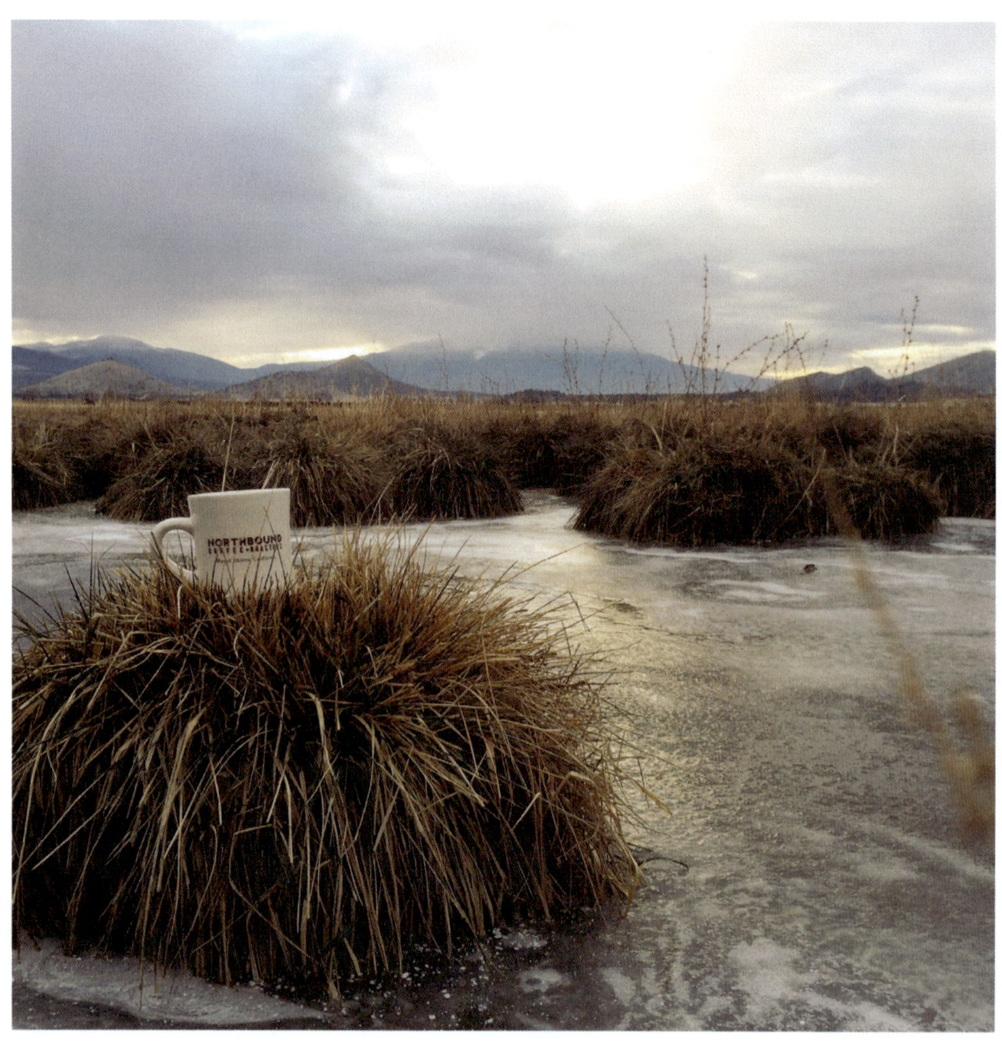

Iced coffee.

Examining something up close—whether it's a flower, a tree, or a bee—can open up a world within a world, so it's essential to slow down and notice the details around you.

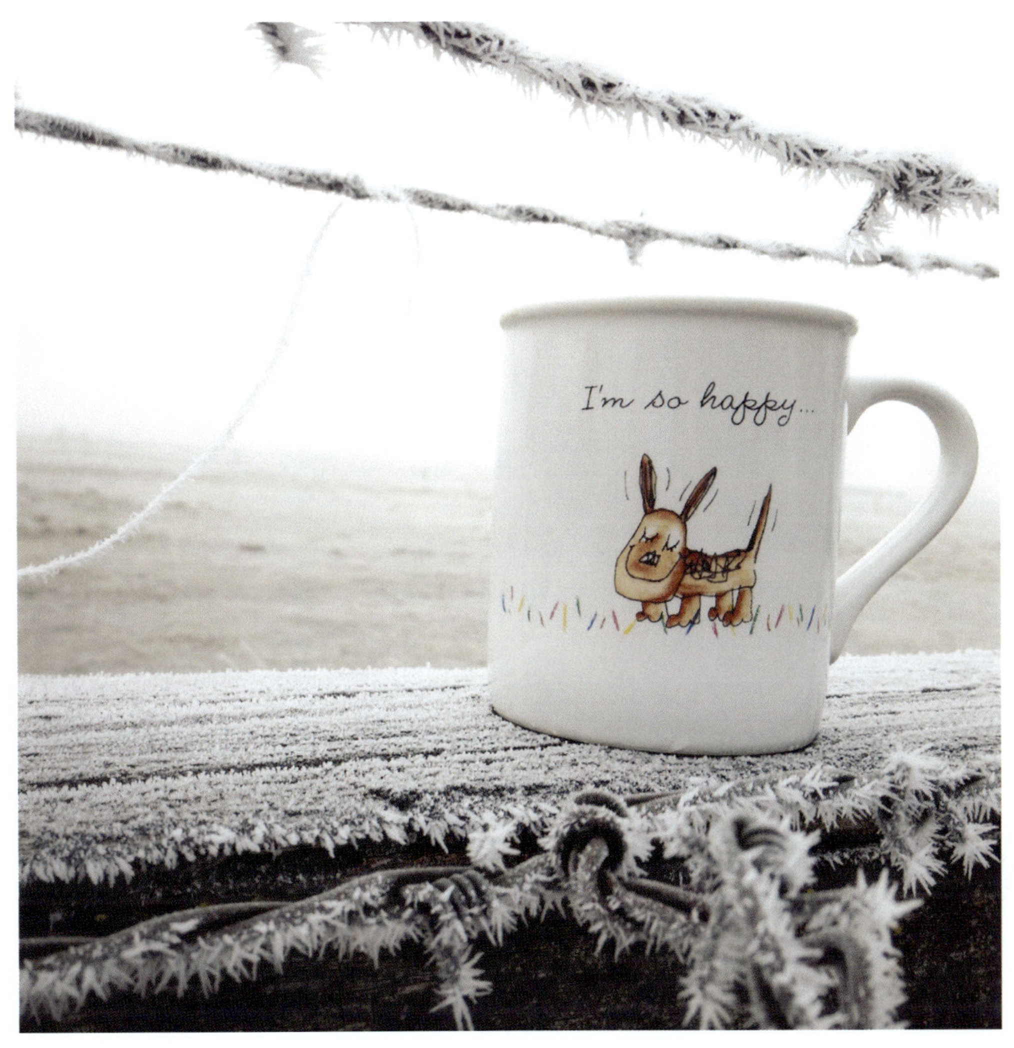

Frosty coffee.

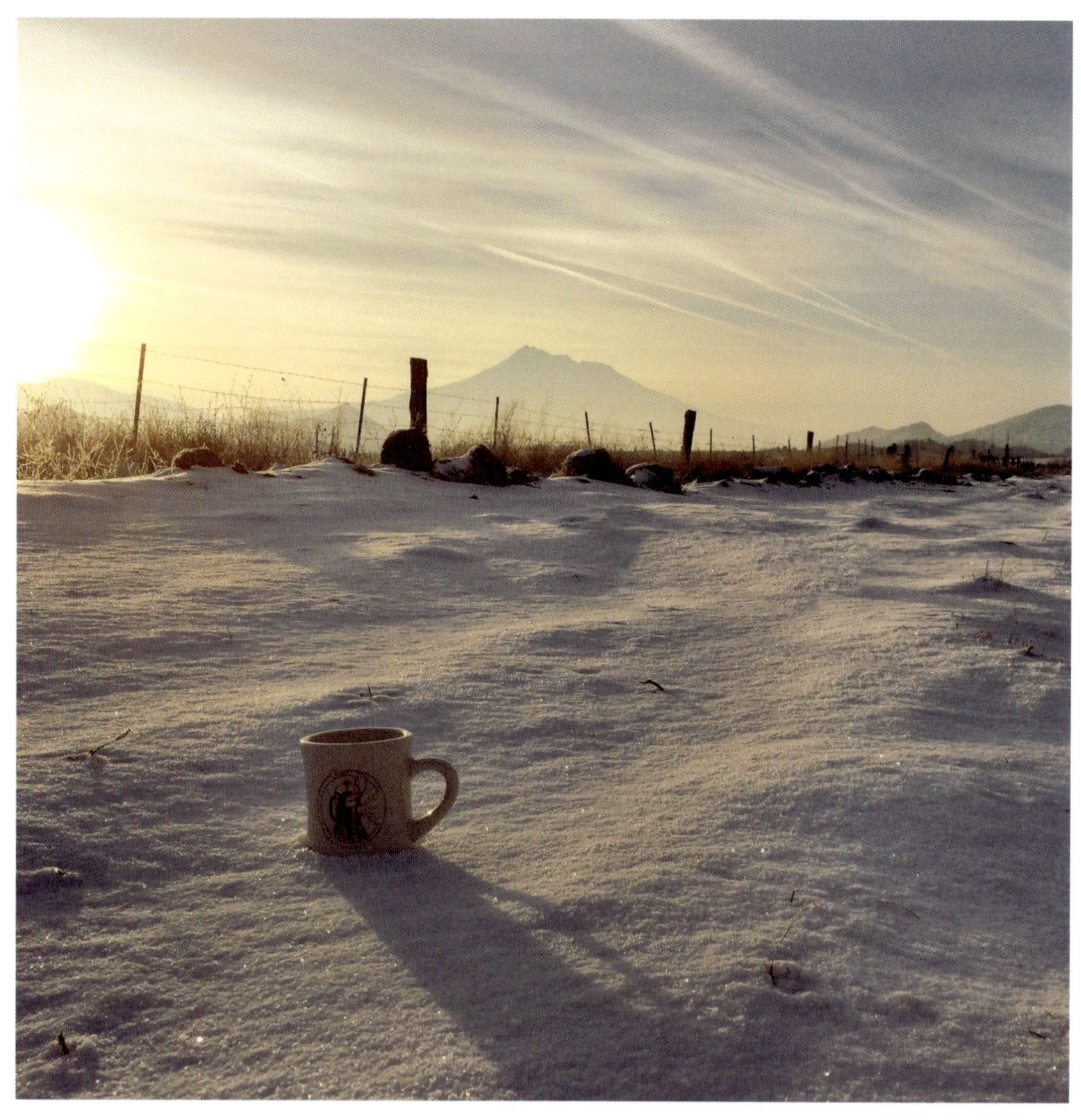

Snowy coffee.

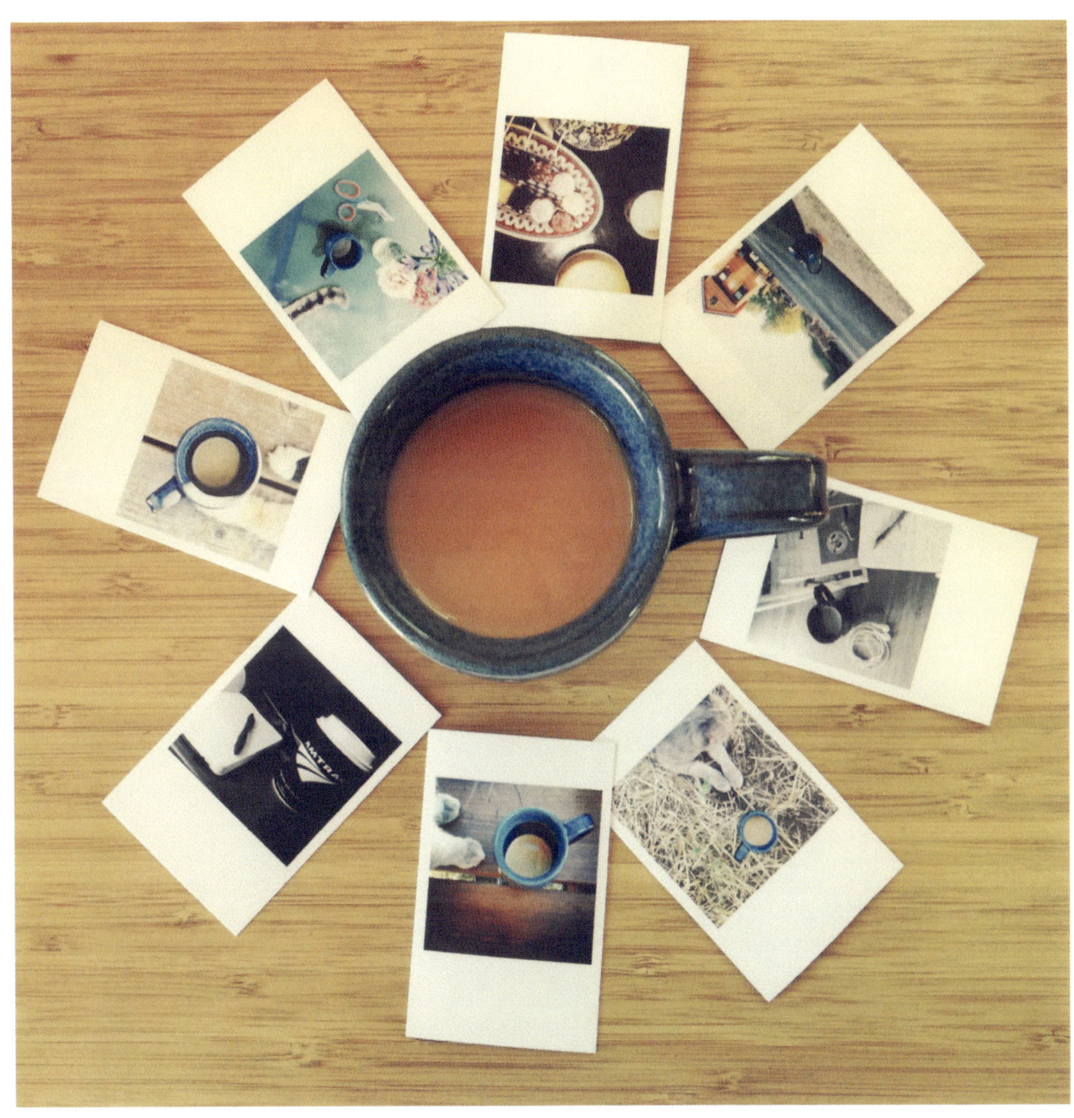

Magical moments.

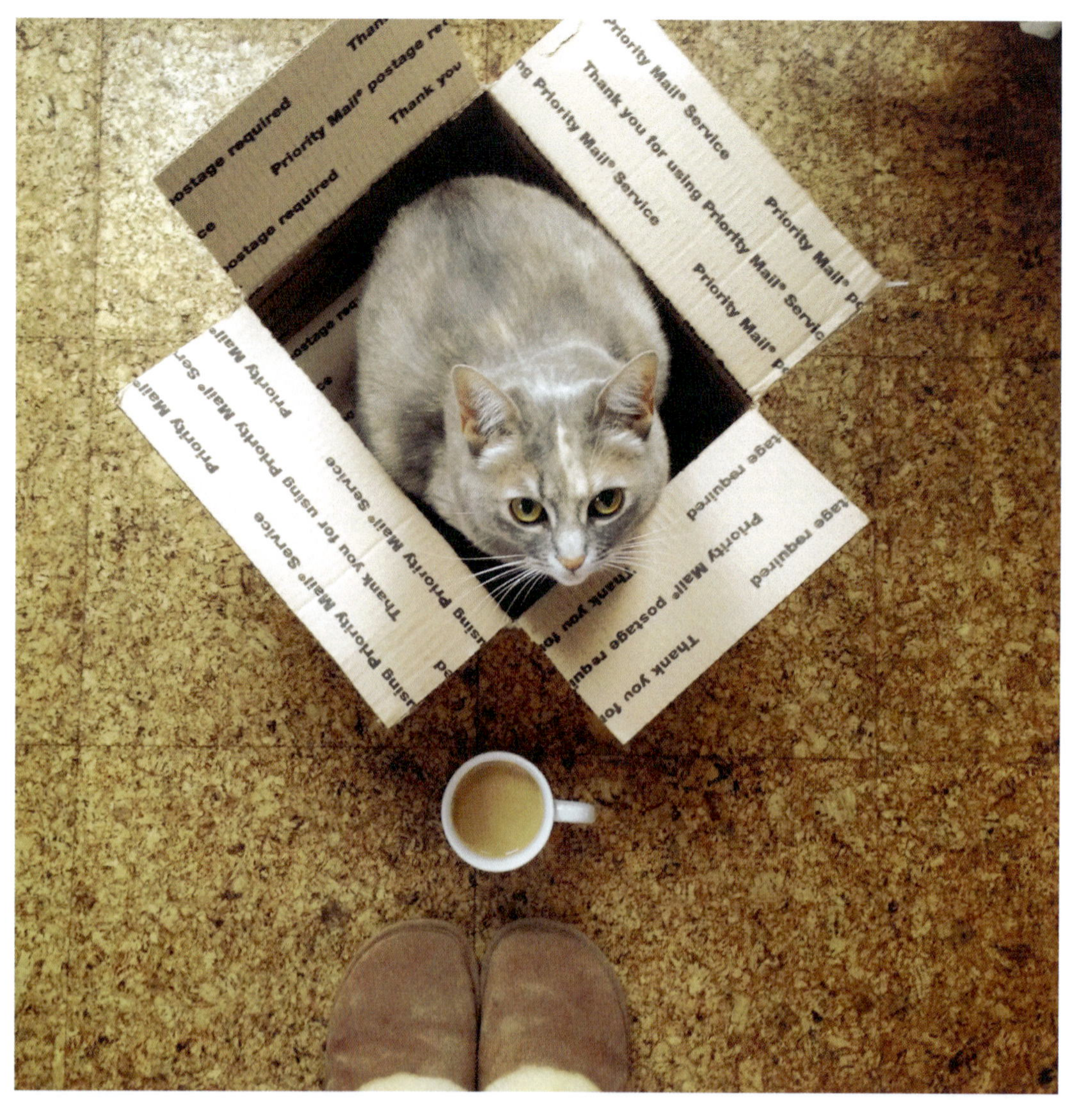

Priority mail.

A box is the perfect cat trap.

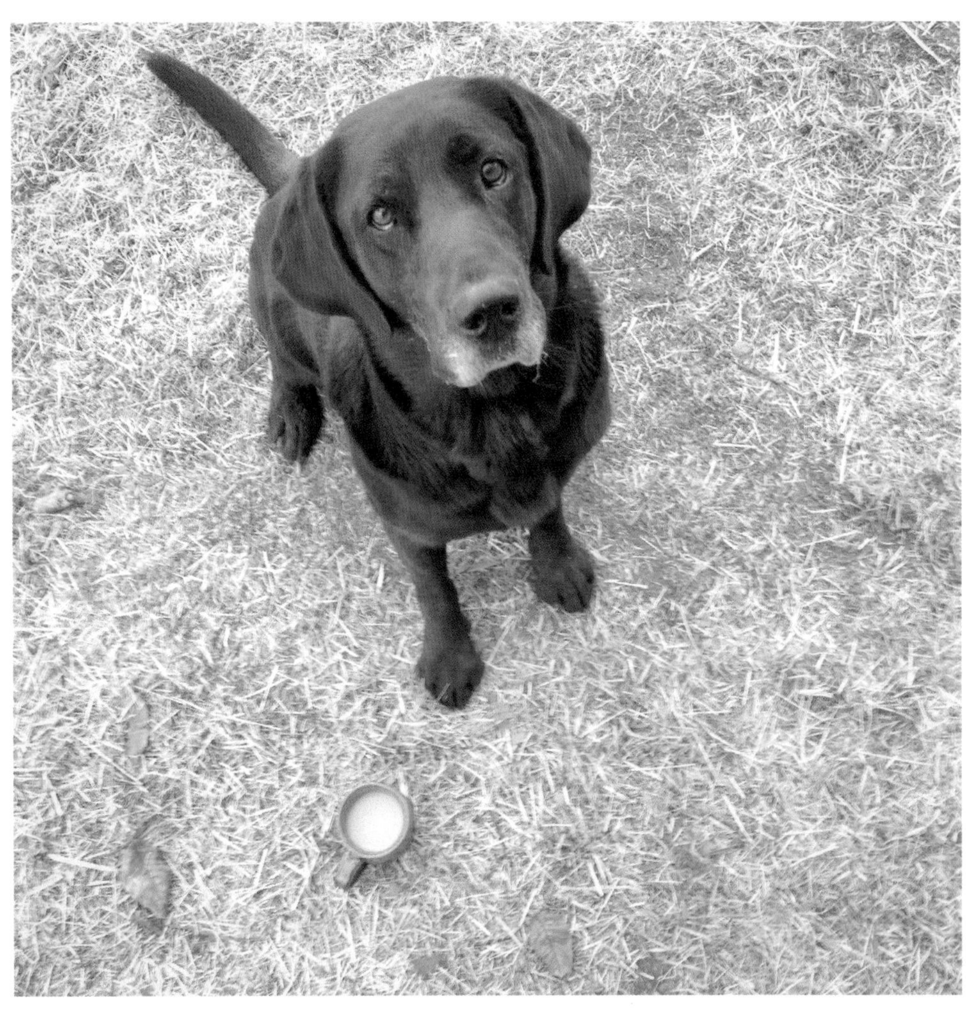

Do you have my ball?

During the summer of 2013, we lived in Chico, California. I started playing fetch with our neighbor's dog, Huck, in the mornings. Huck got used to the routine, and when I woke up I would find him waiting patiently for me on our porch. Huck worshipped his tennis ball and loved playing in the early morning hours.

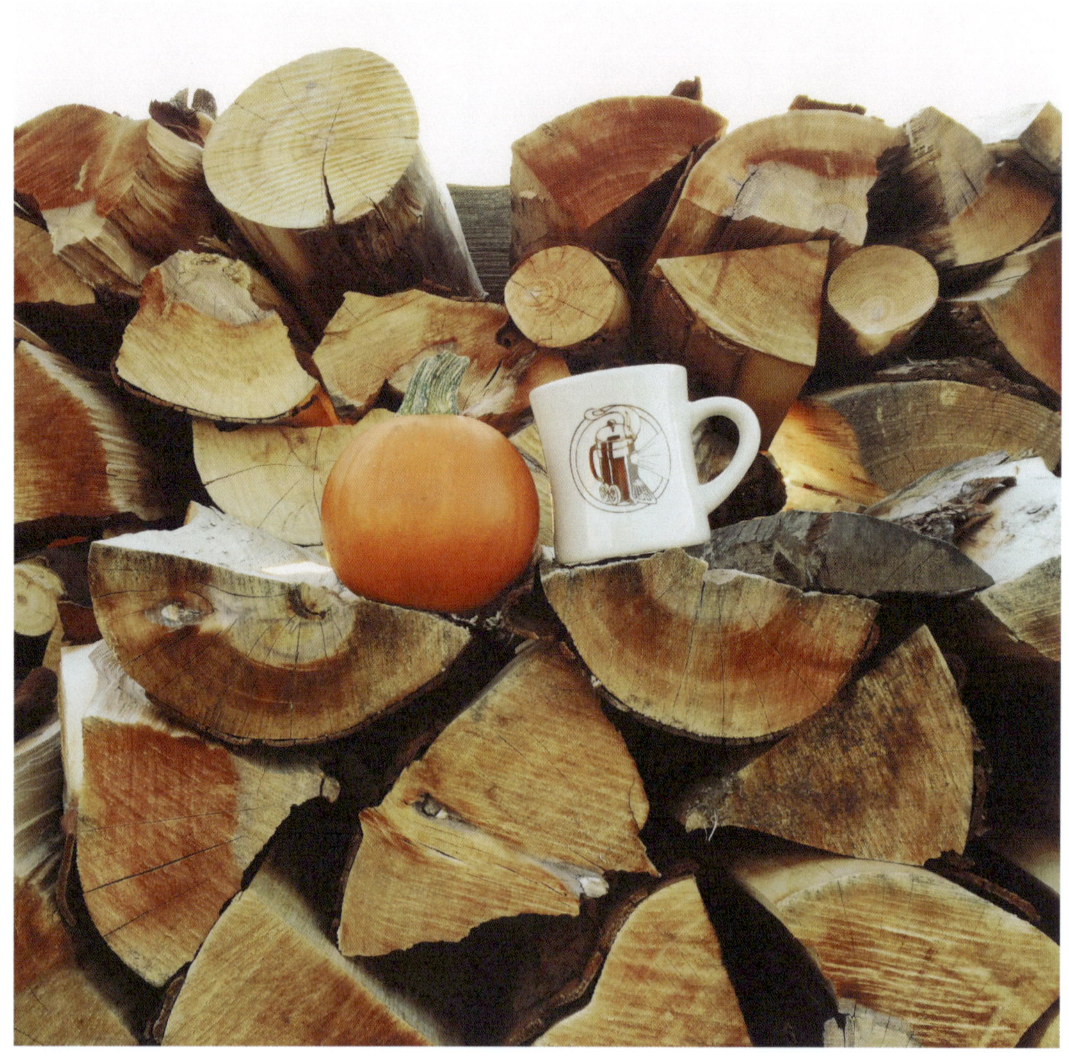

Happy Halloween!

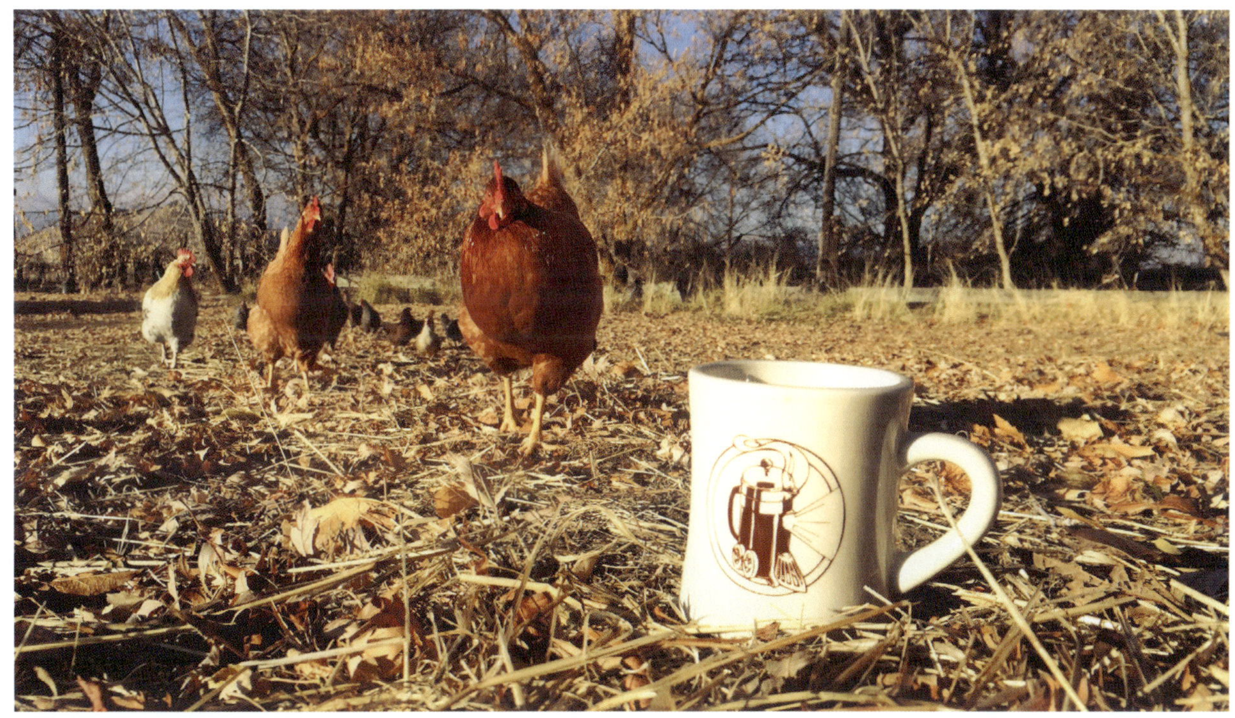

Chickens are curious creatures.

I set my coffee cup down in leaves to take this shot. I thought it would be cute to have the coffee cup in the foreground and the chickens in the background, but that's not the way it turned out. As soon as I set my coffee cup down, the chickens ran over to me. They were incredibly curious about what I was doing, and you never know, they might like coffee too.

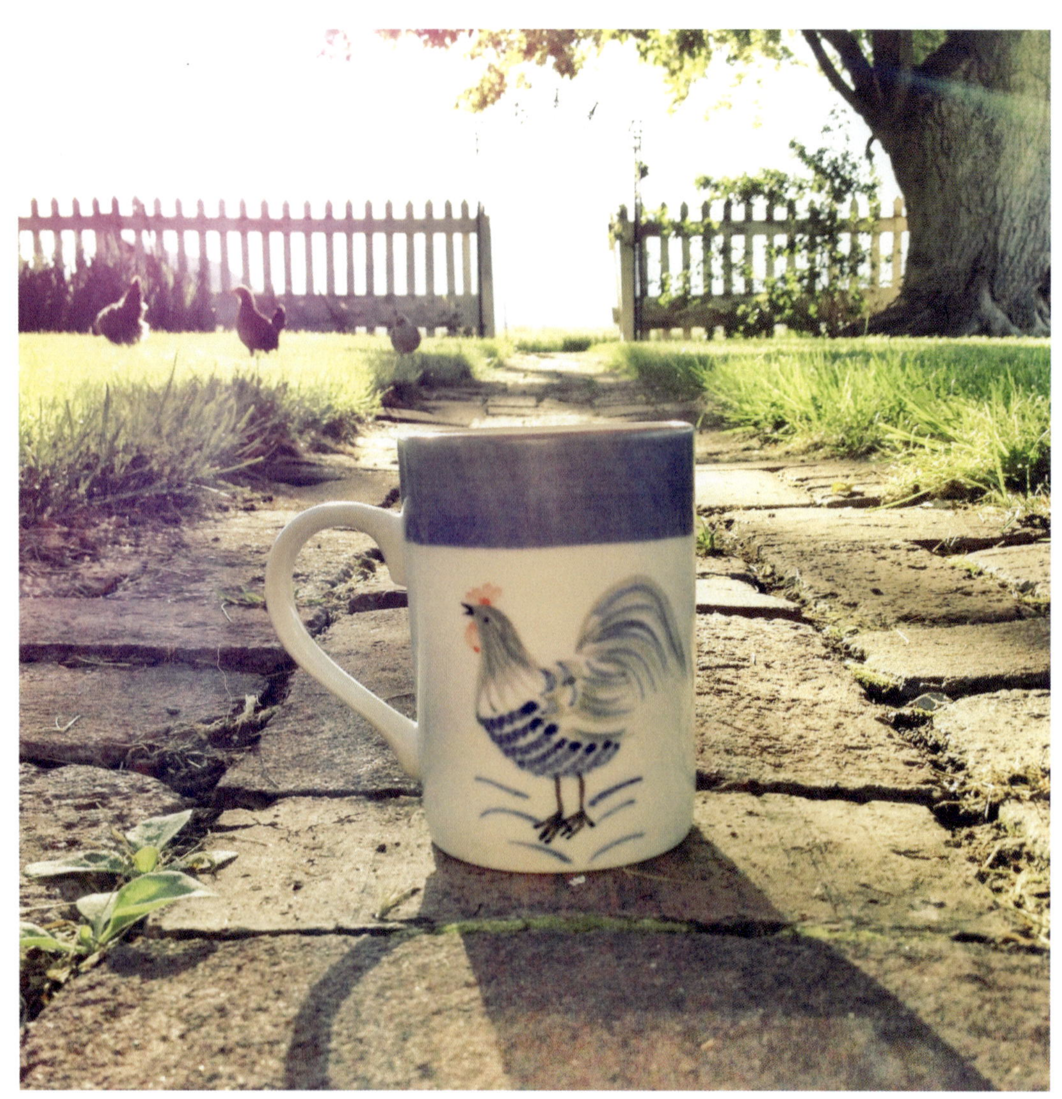

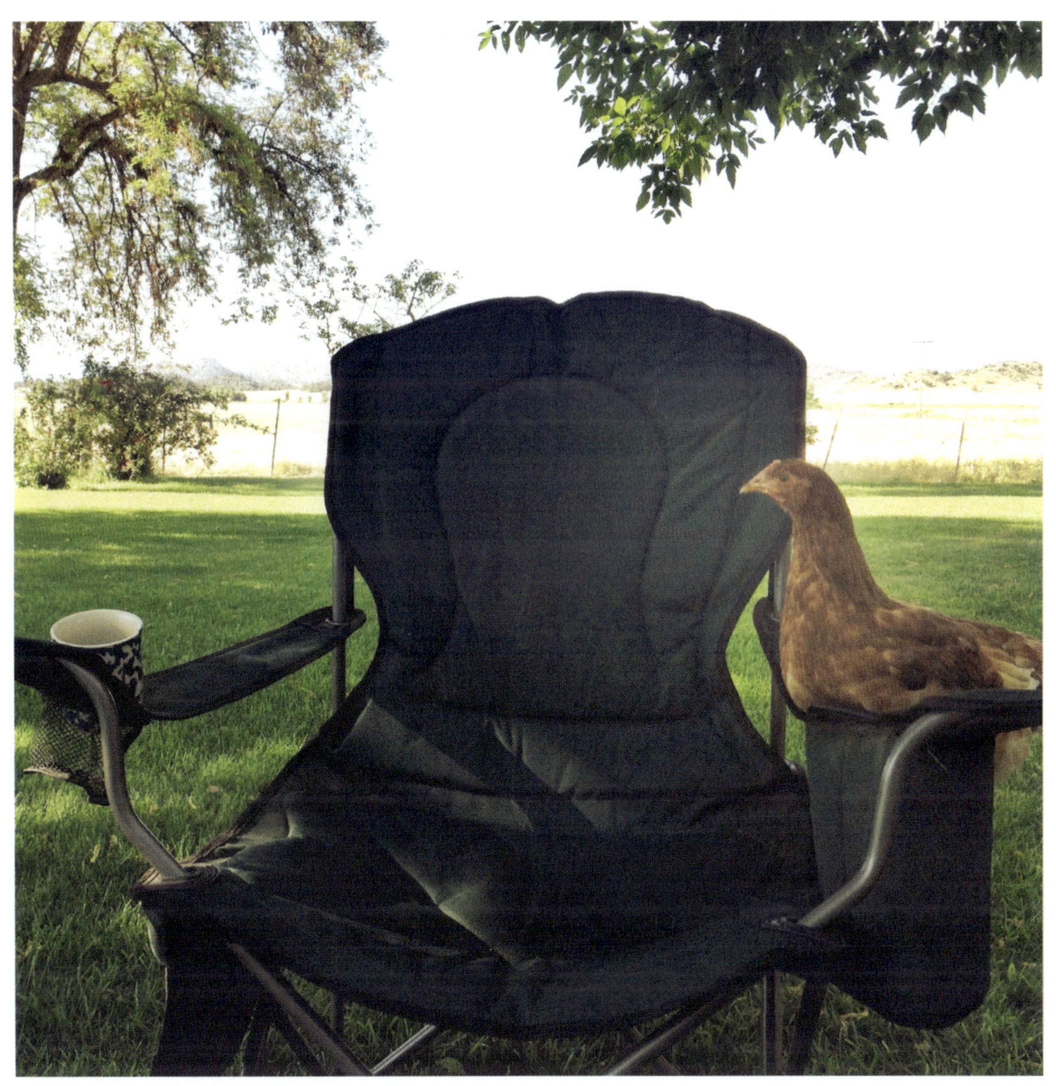

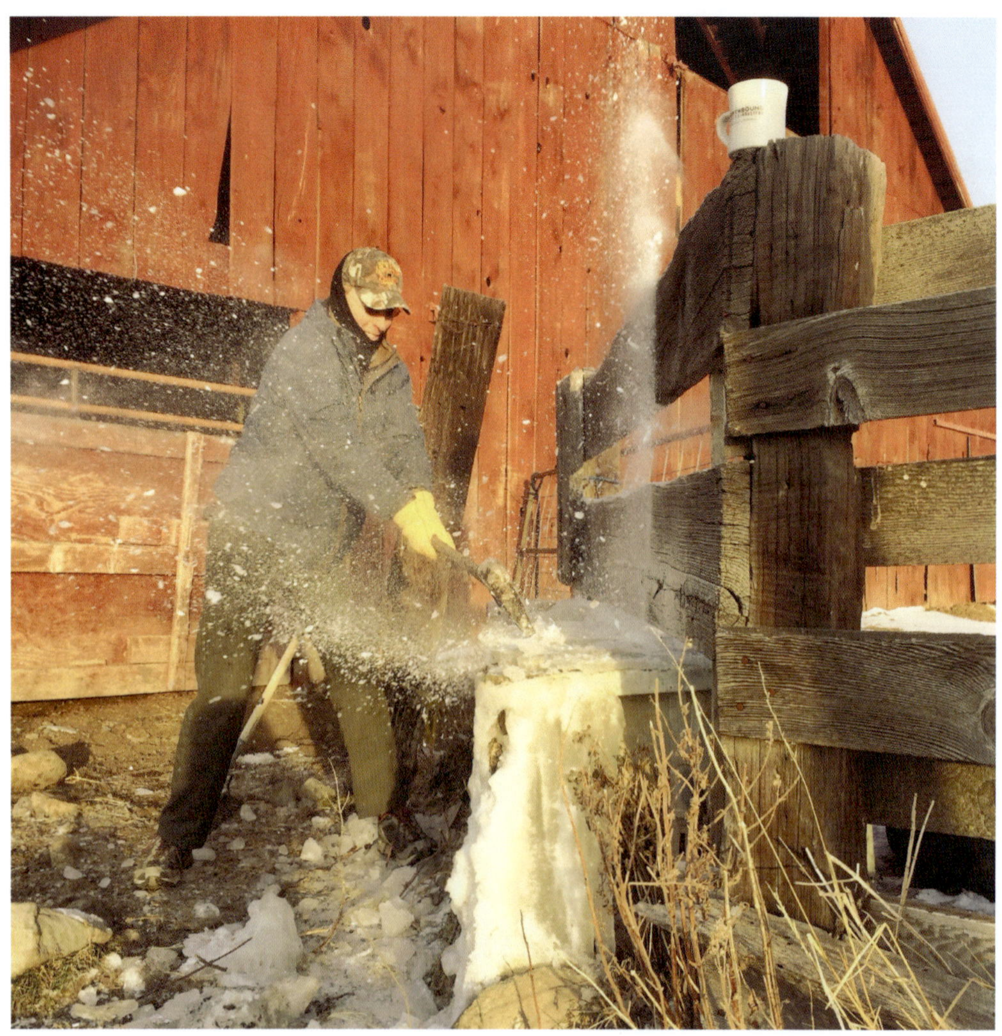

Breaking the ice.

In this image, Logan is breaking the horse's water. It was early December 2013 and we had a cold snap come through the valley. The weather broke numerous records in the area and the lowest low was -9 degrees F.

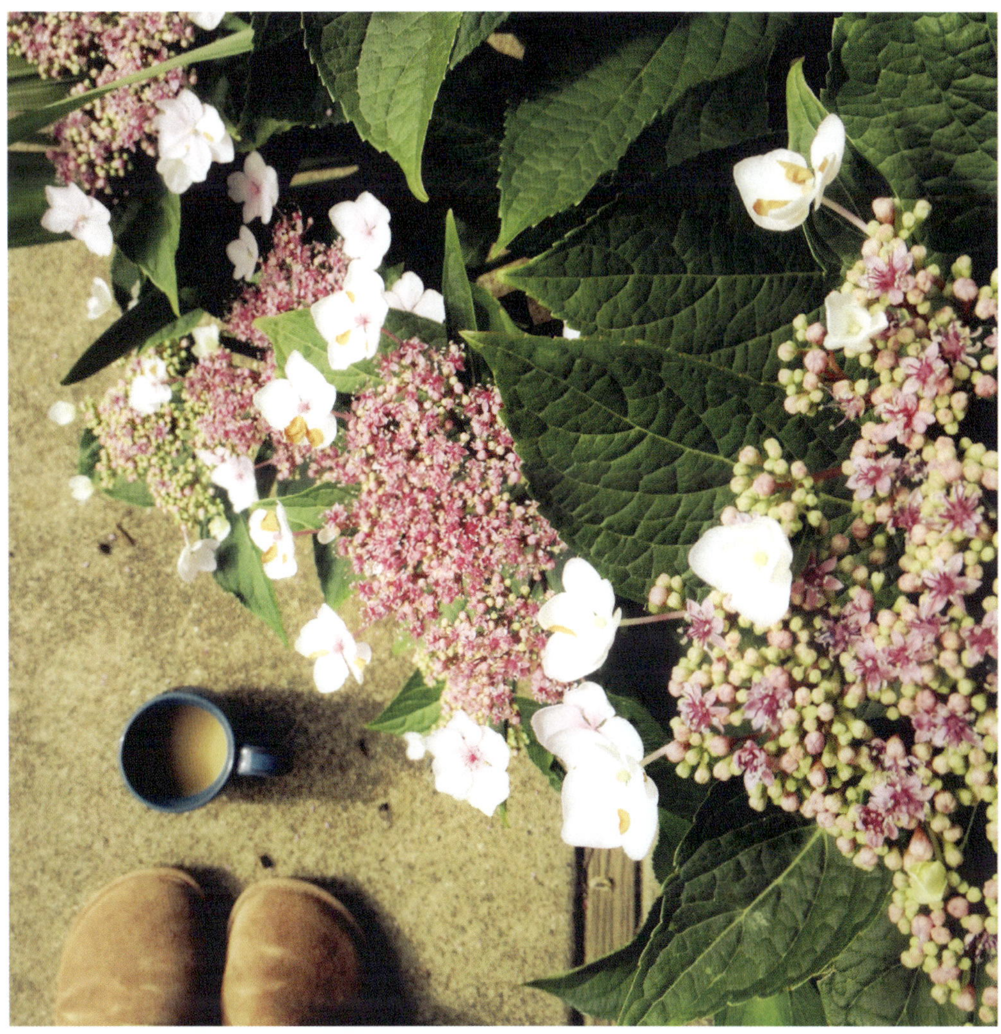

From where I stand.

Look for patterns in leaves, in trees, and in the clouds above you. Patterns can give photos structure, texture, and a sense of place. If you have a hard time finding patterns, look up, down, and around you. Patterns are everywhere.

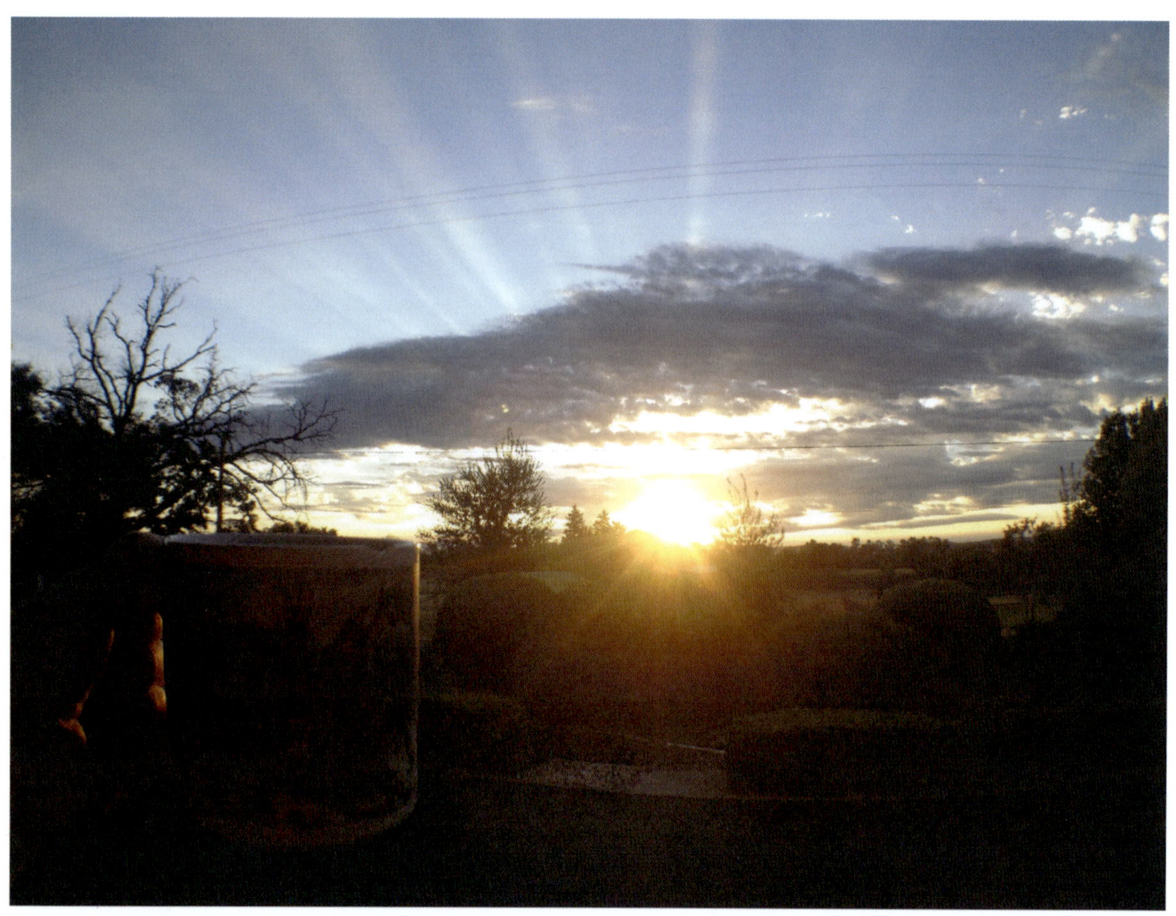

Red Bluff sunrise.

Depending on the type of light you work with, a photo can convey a sense of peace, joy, or even foreboding. Learn as much as possible about different lighting scenarios, and you will capture beautiful images and tell stories with your photos. For example, sunrise and sunset are wonderful times of day to take photos. The light is soft and the colors are stunning, which explains why I love to take my photo walks at these times of day. Every day, I notice something new about the landscape because the light and the clouds are constantly changing.

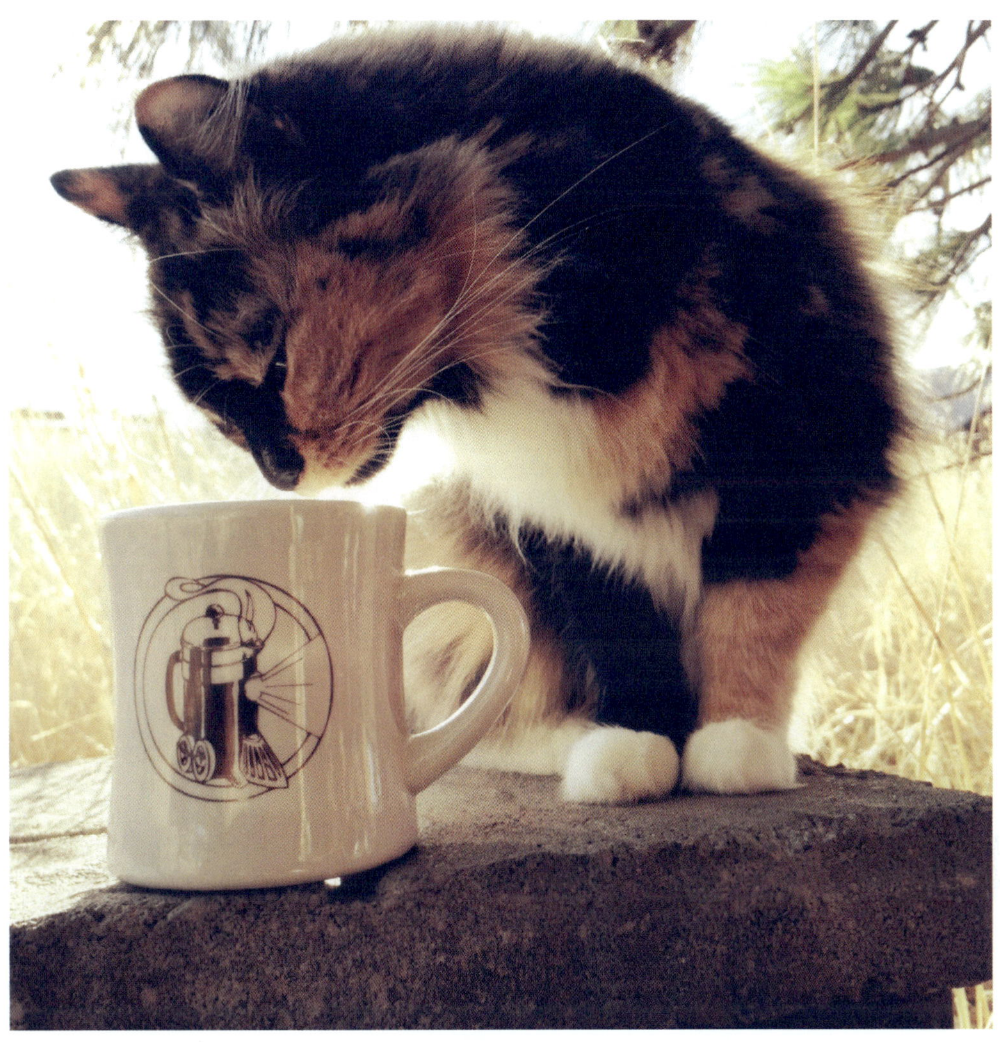

Cupping cat.

As you shoot, think about what is in the foreground and background. A good way to do this is to find leading lines. Every photo has the potential to be full of linear elements, like roads, ridgelines, or tree branches. How you can artfully incorporate these lines to frame the subject of your photo?

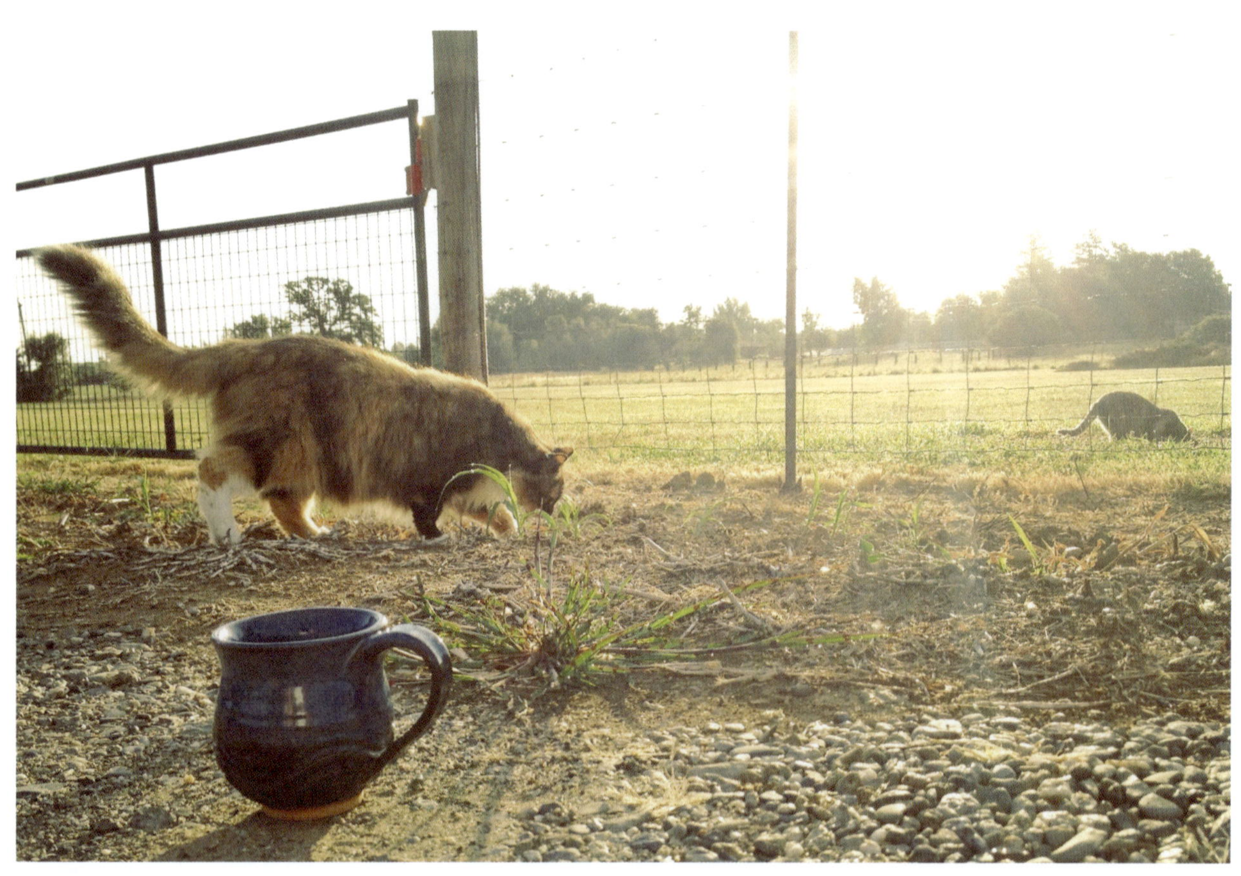

Grazing cats.

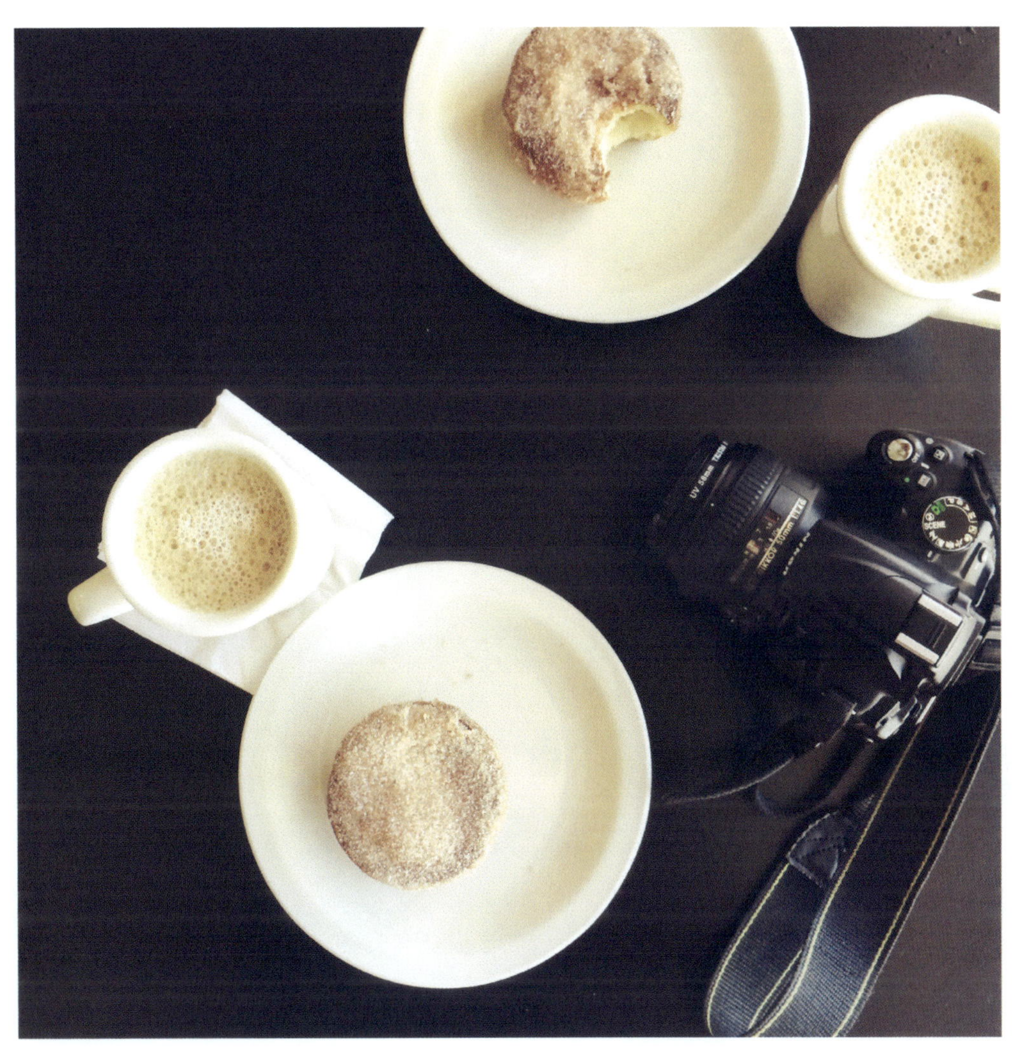

Mt. Shasta pastry.

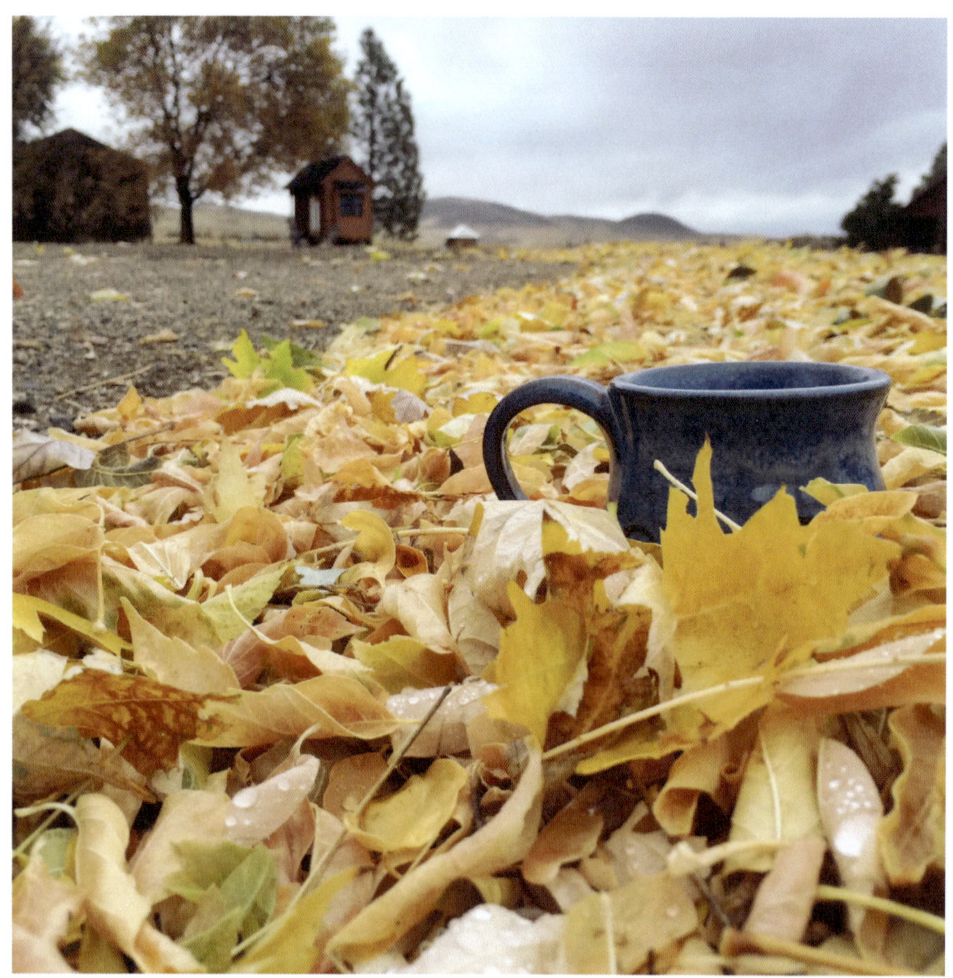

Perspective.

"It's a powerful thing to use our viewfinders to picture the world around us. Photography provides us with the perfect way to express ourselves . . . With each image, no matter the subject at hand, we illuminate what matters most to us, and that is not only inspiring, it's transformative."

— Tracey Clark

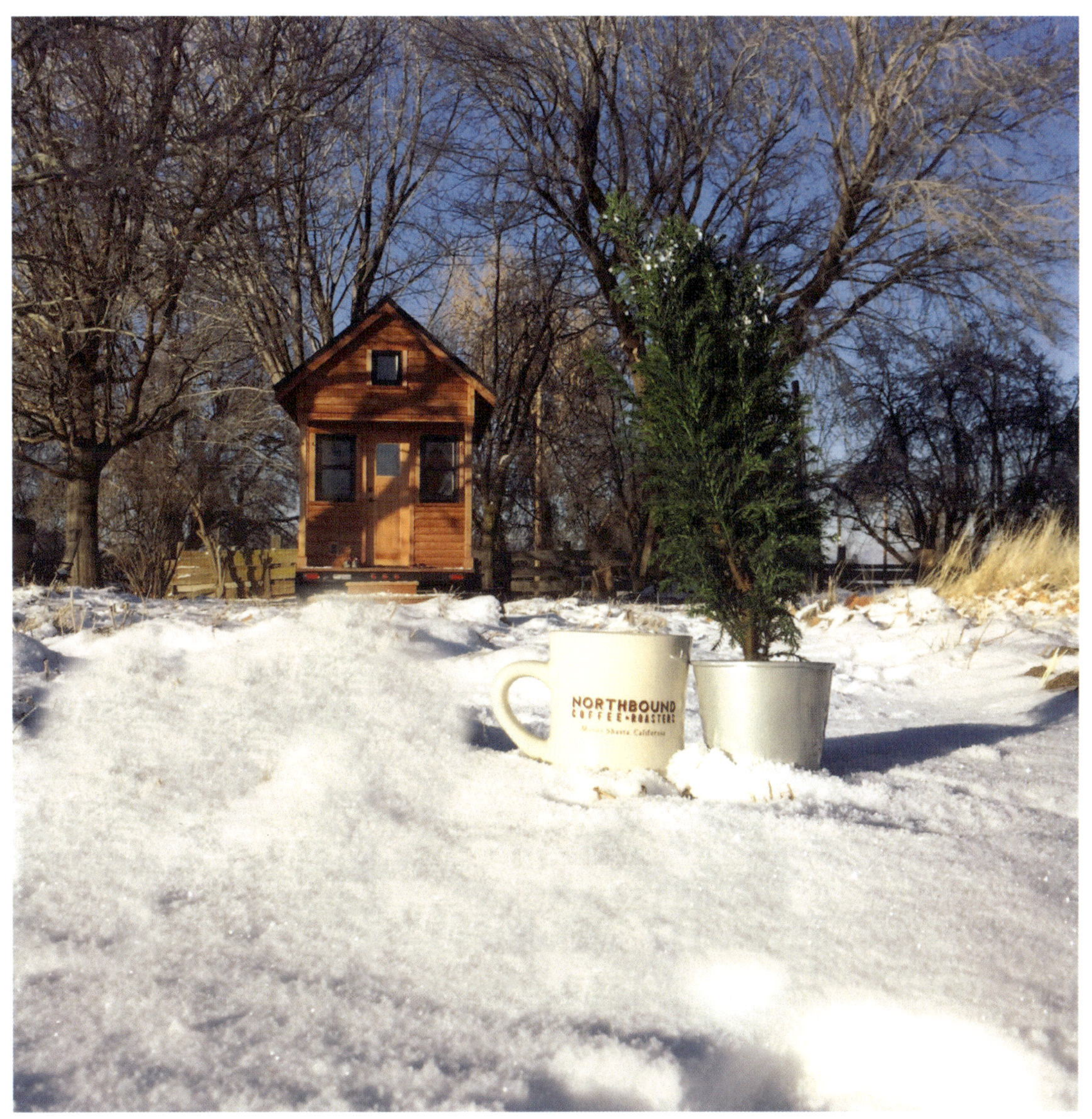
NORTHBOUND
COFFEE • ROASTERS

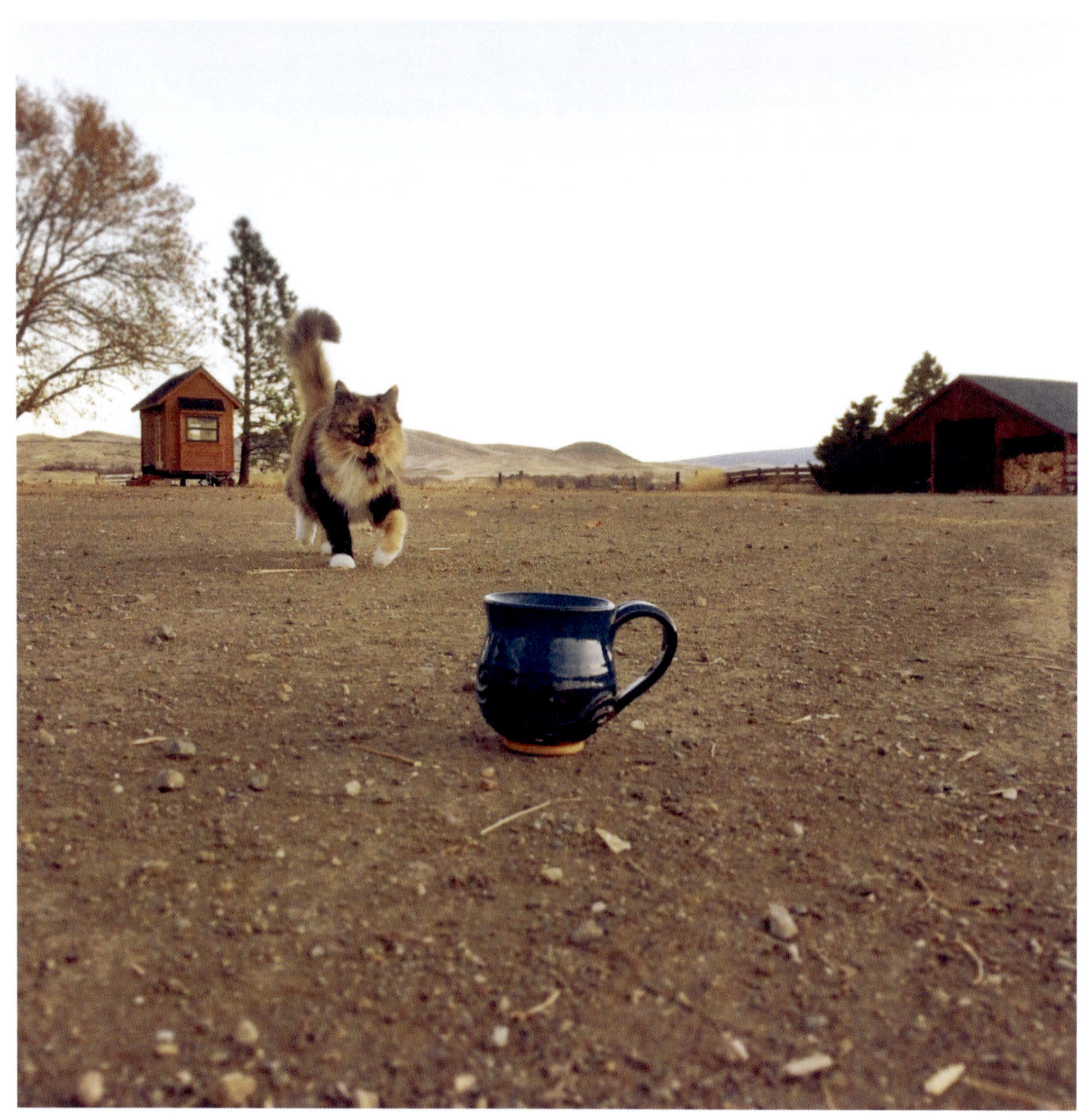

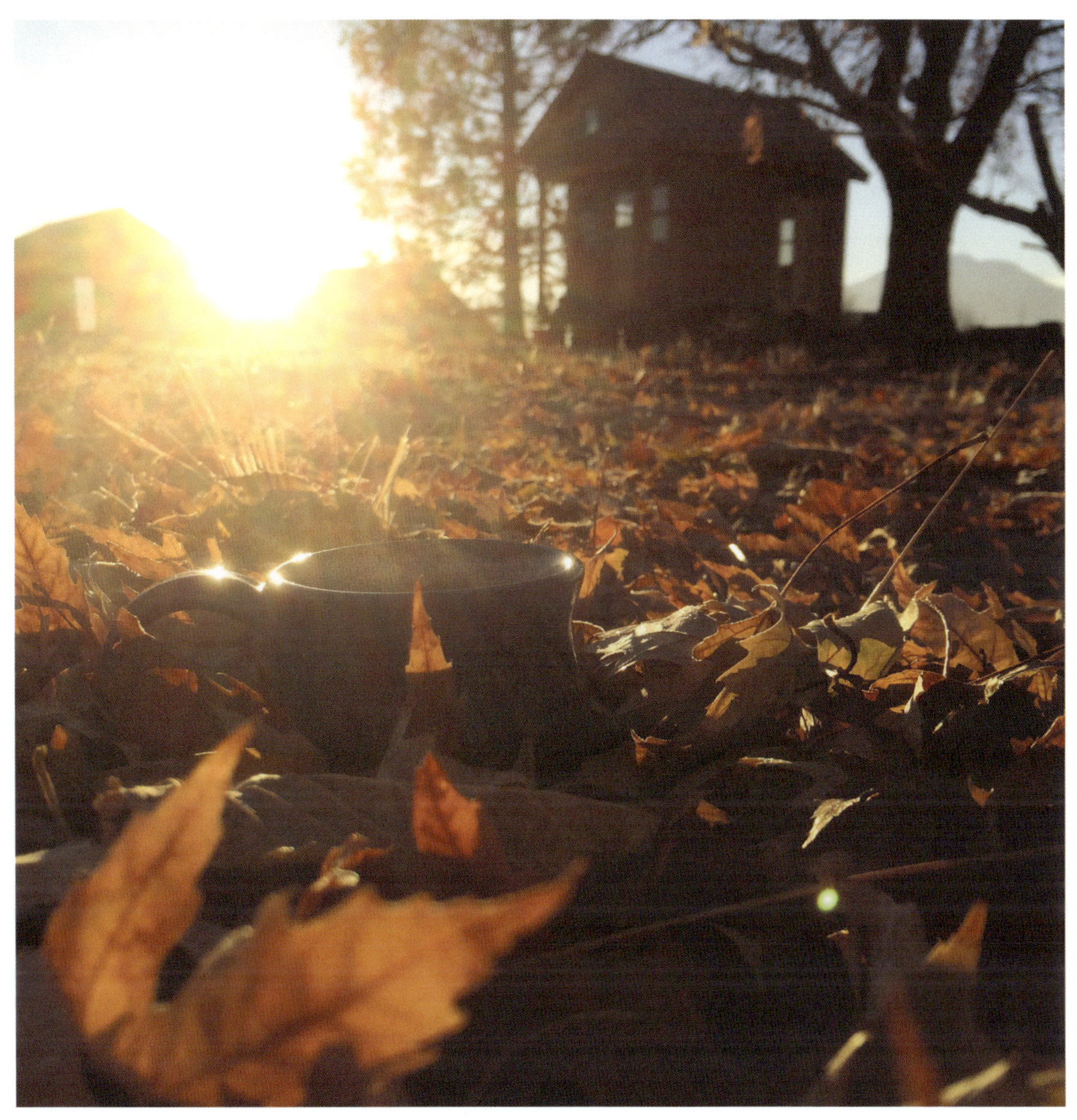

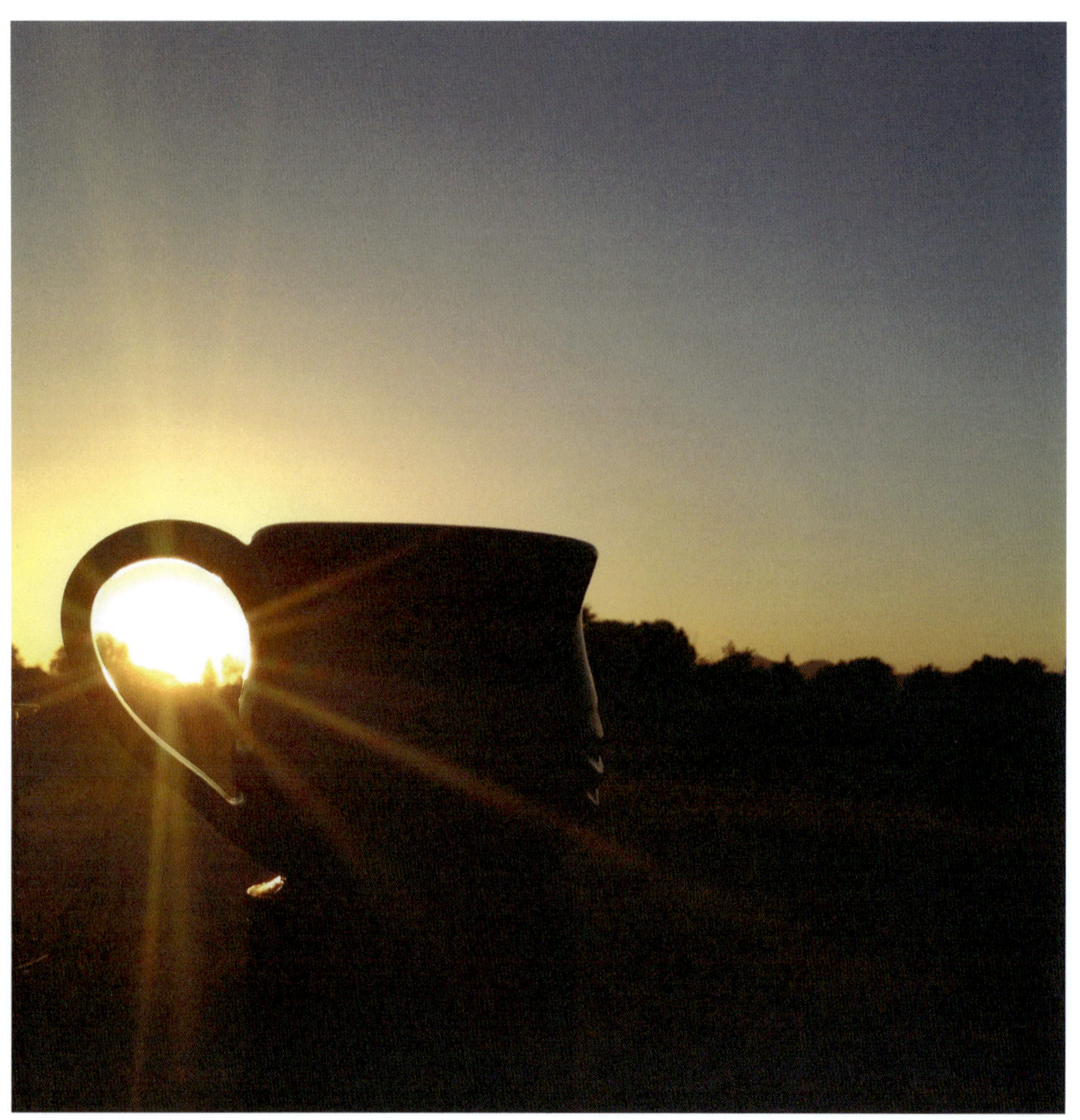

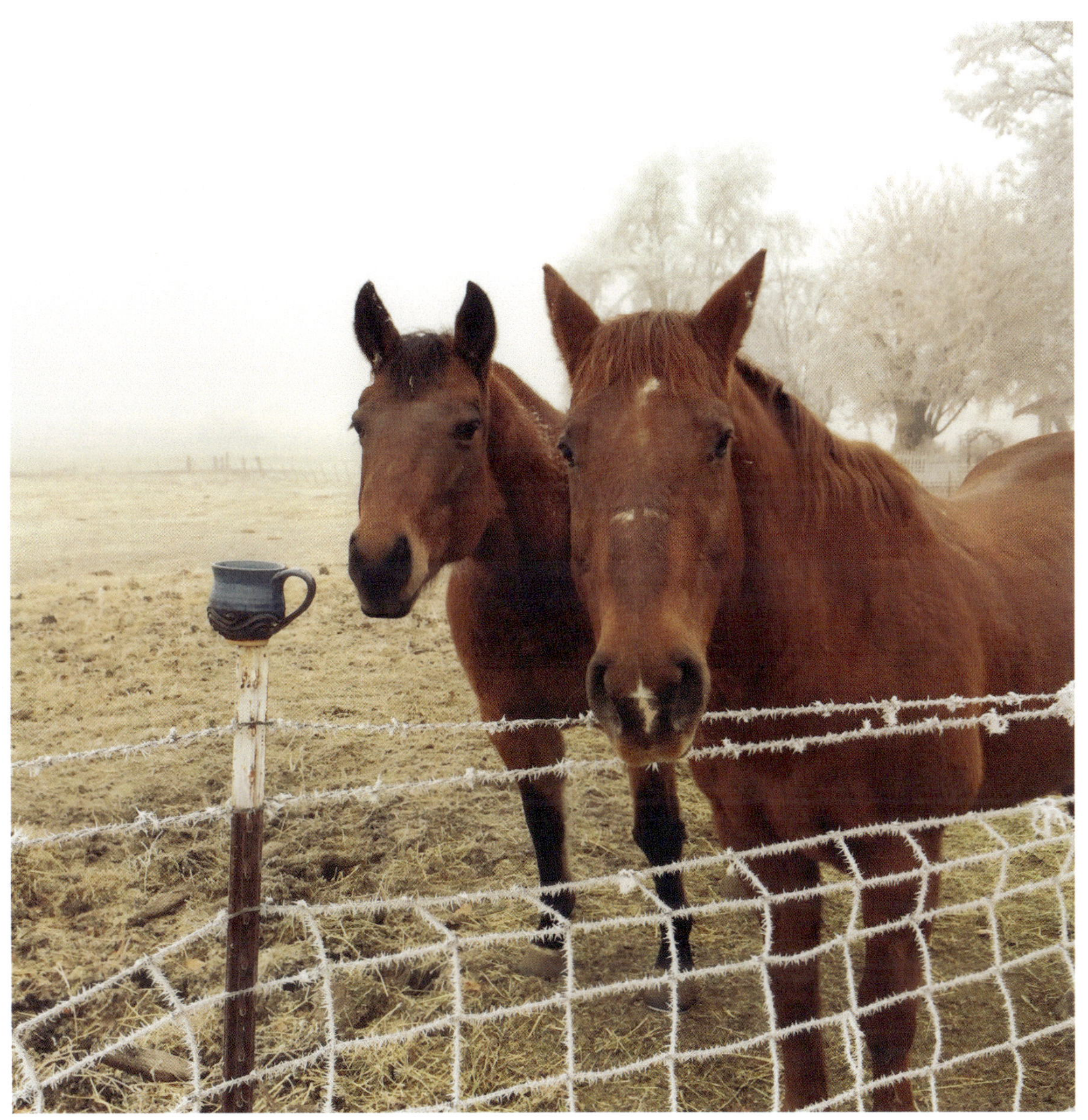

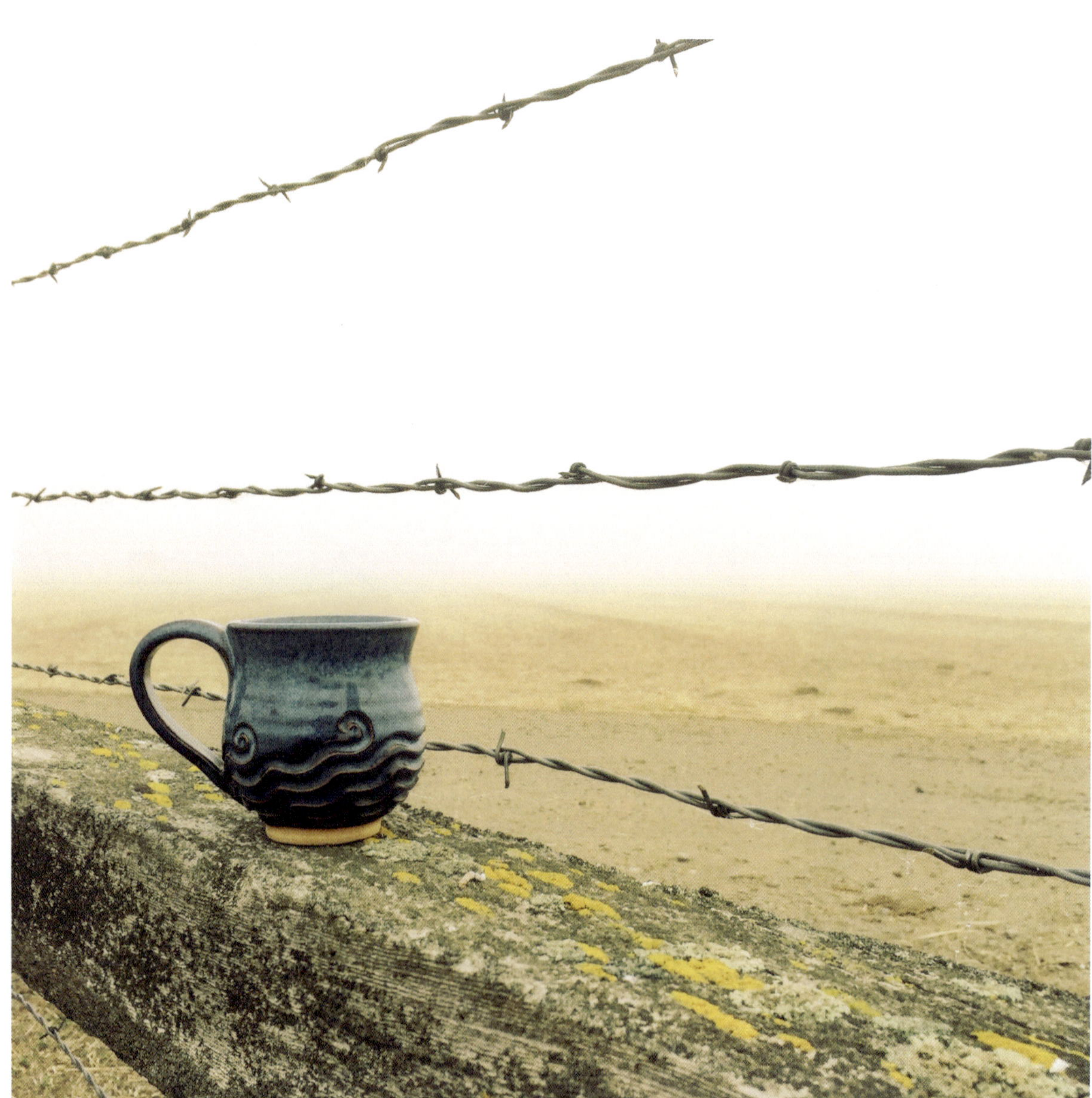

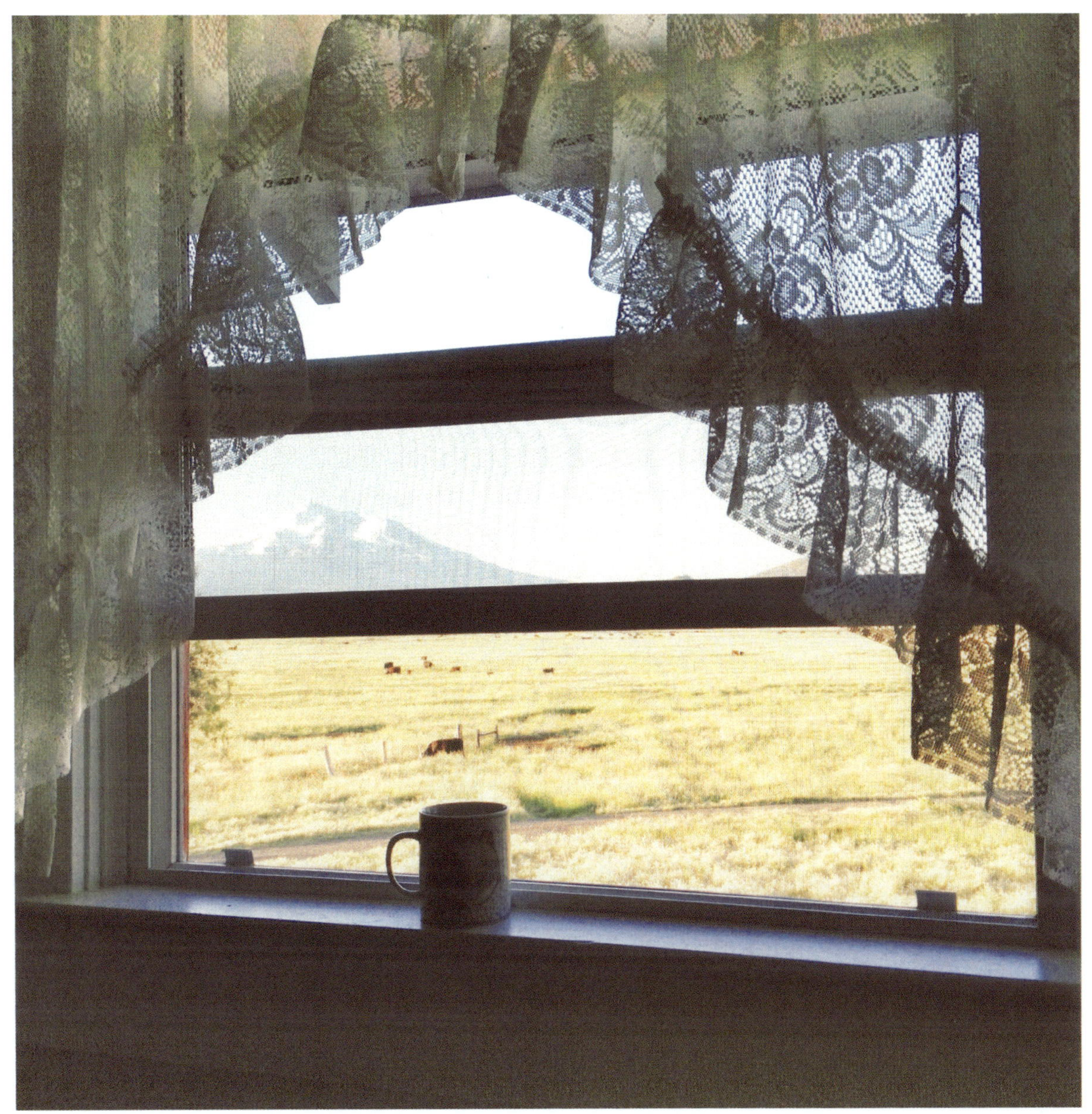

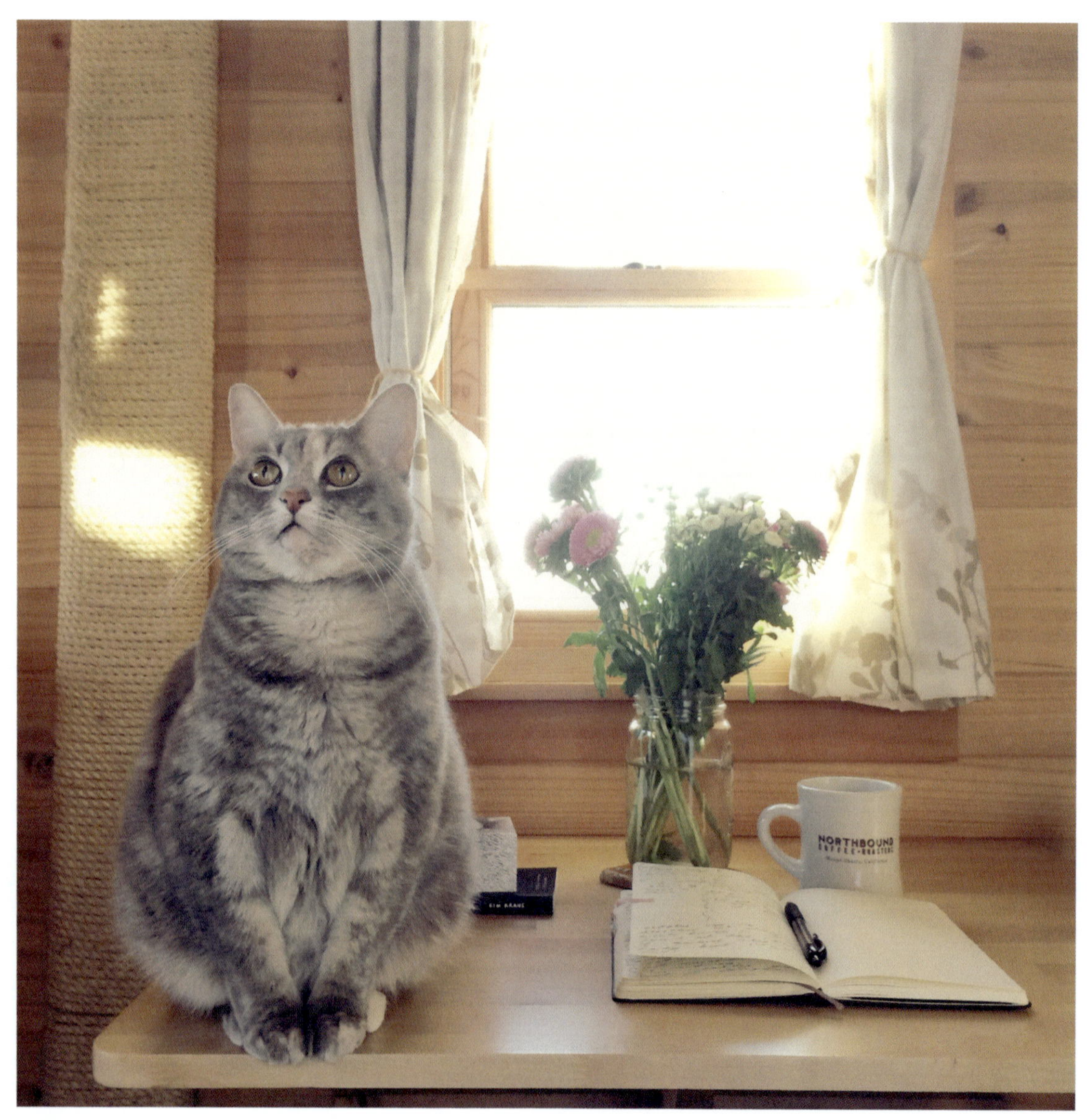

Morning pages.

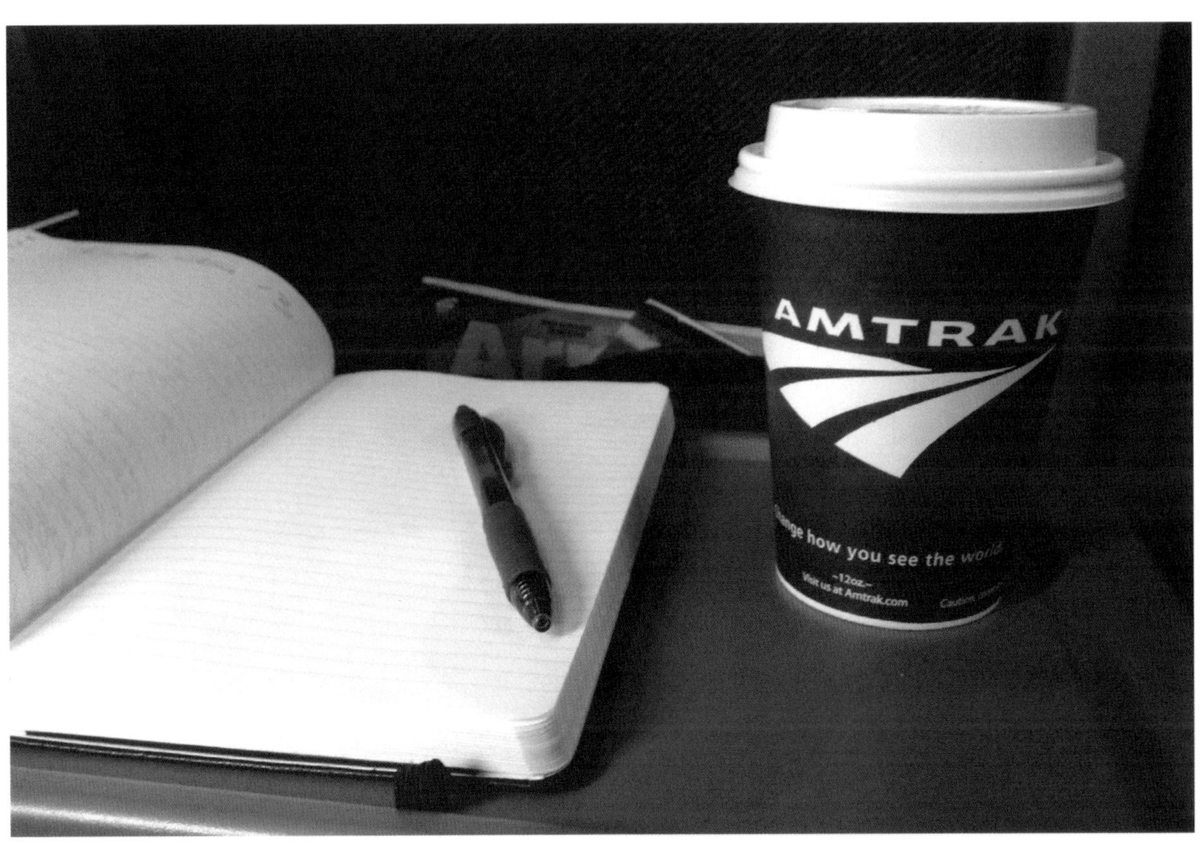
AMTRAK
Visit us at Amtrak.com

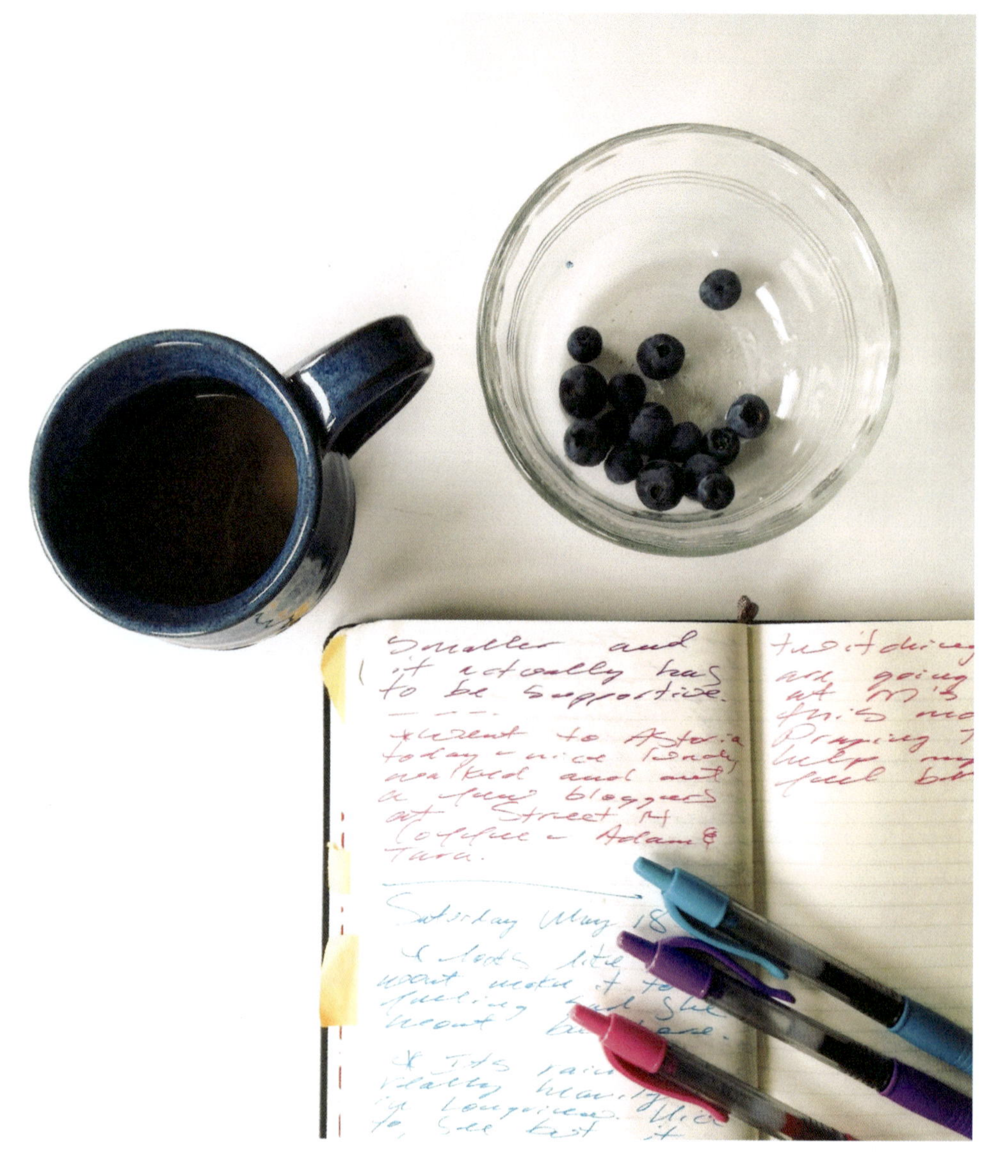
Smaller and
it actually has
to be supportive.
Went to Astoria
today - nice Sunday,
walked and met
a few bloggers
at Street 14
Coffee - Adam &
Tara.
Saturday May 18

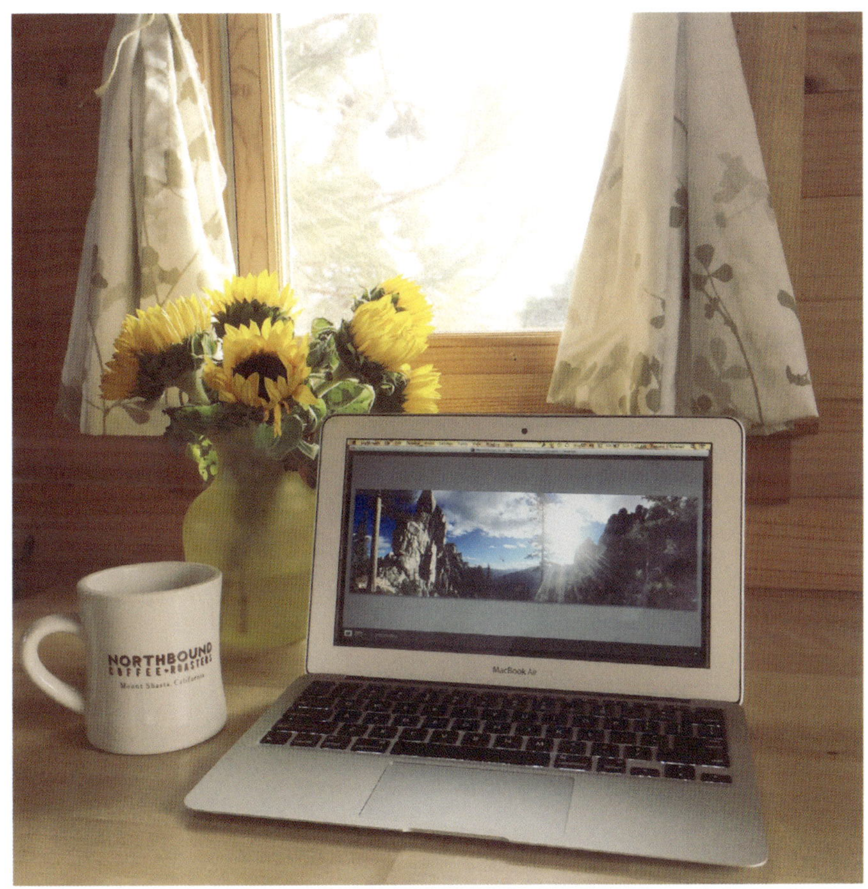

Editing.

Processing your digital photos can be as much fun as taking them. Depending on the software, there are hundreds of processing options to choose from, which can be thrilling, but also overwhelming. Software programs allow you to adjust the temperature and brightness, which can help evoke a mood in the photo. Sometimes I make dramatic adjustments to my photos, and other times I don't process my images at all. Even if you decide to forgo processing your images, I recommend using the sharpening tool because it brings out details that might go unnoticed.

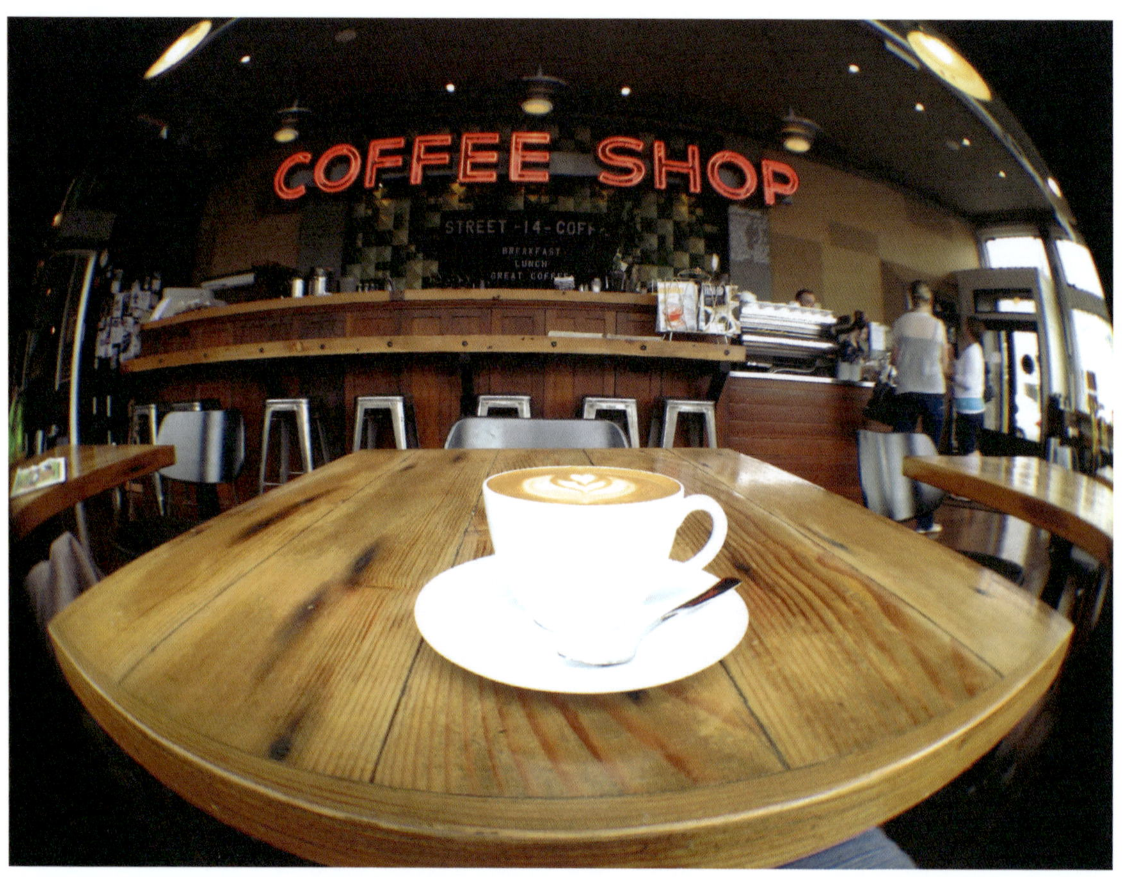

Coffee shop.

As you look through your viewfinder, pretend you are looking through a grid. The grid will have two horizontal lines and two vertical lines, leaving you with nine sections. This grid is used in the rule of thirds. It's useful to understand because it gives you control over the proportions in the image you shoot. Remember, rules are helpful, but they aren't everything. Sometimes it's more fun to put the main subject off to the side, rather than in the center of the frame. The most important thing you can do is visualize an image before you take a photo. Don't be afraid to try new things. You might need to lie on the ground or crouch low to get the perfect picture. Just go for it. Experiment and have fun.

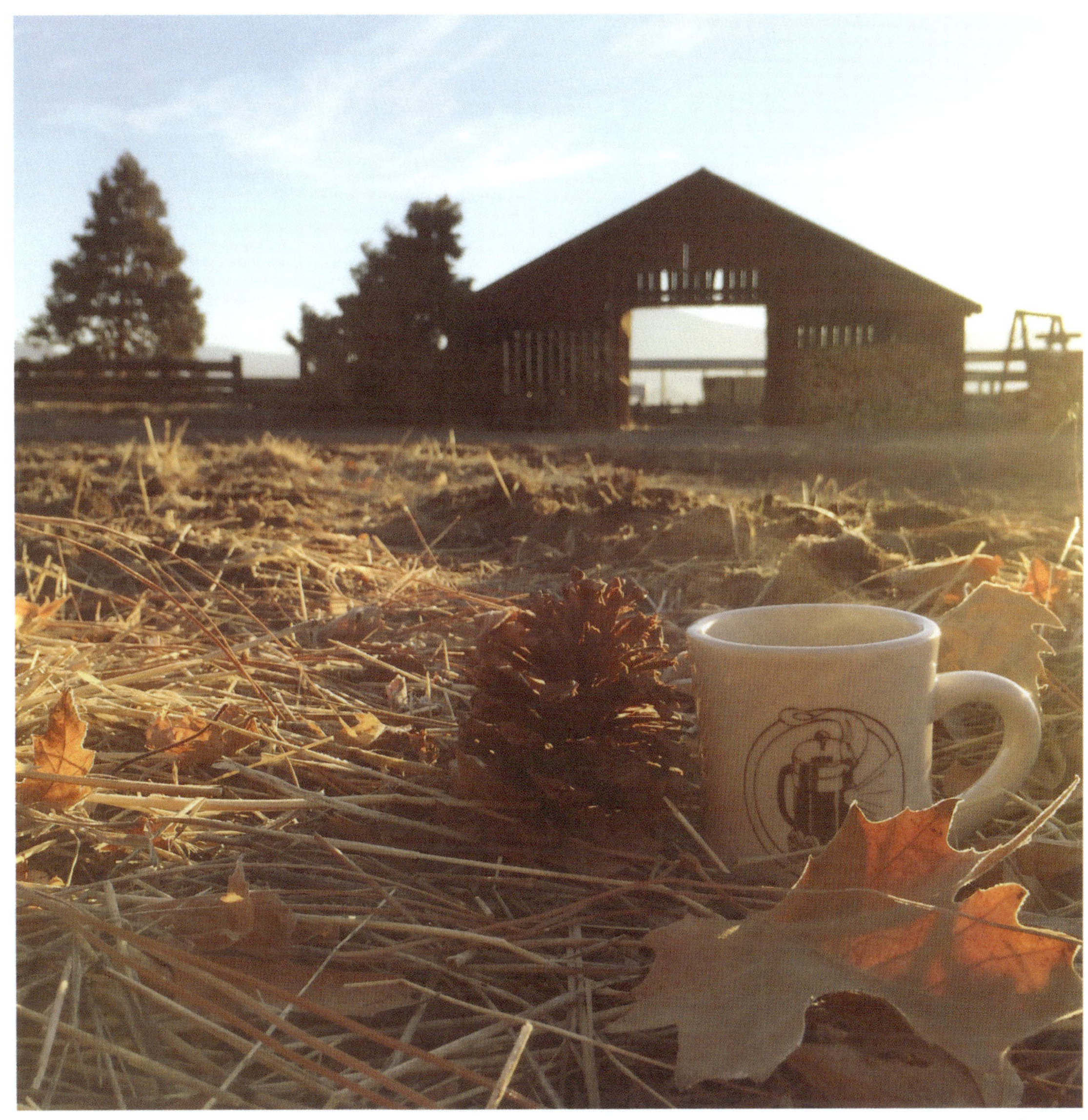

Fall colors.

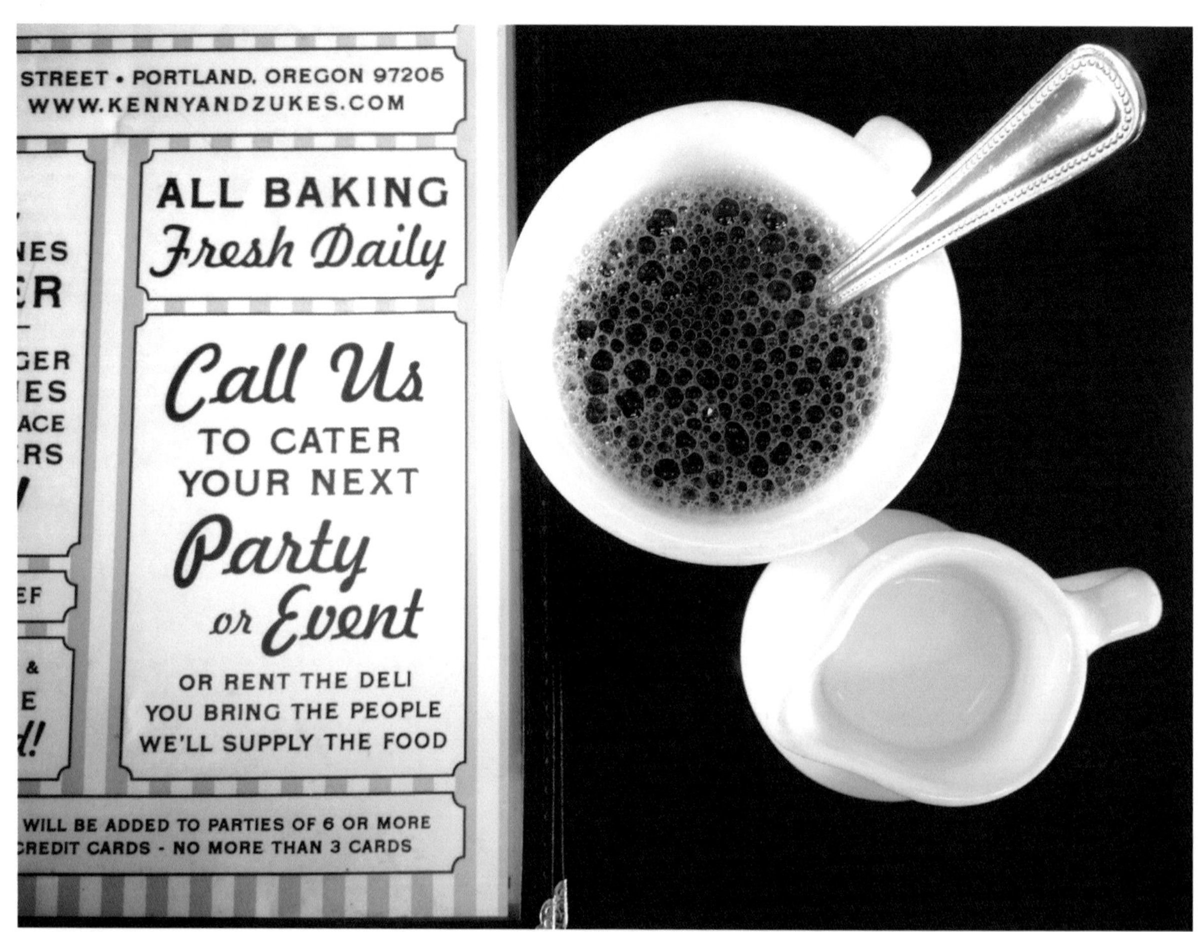

Portland adventures.

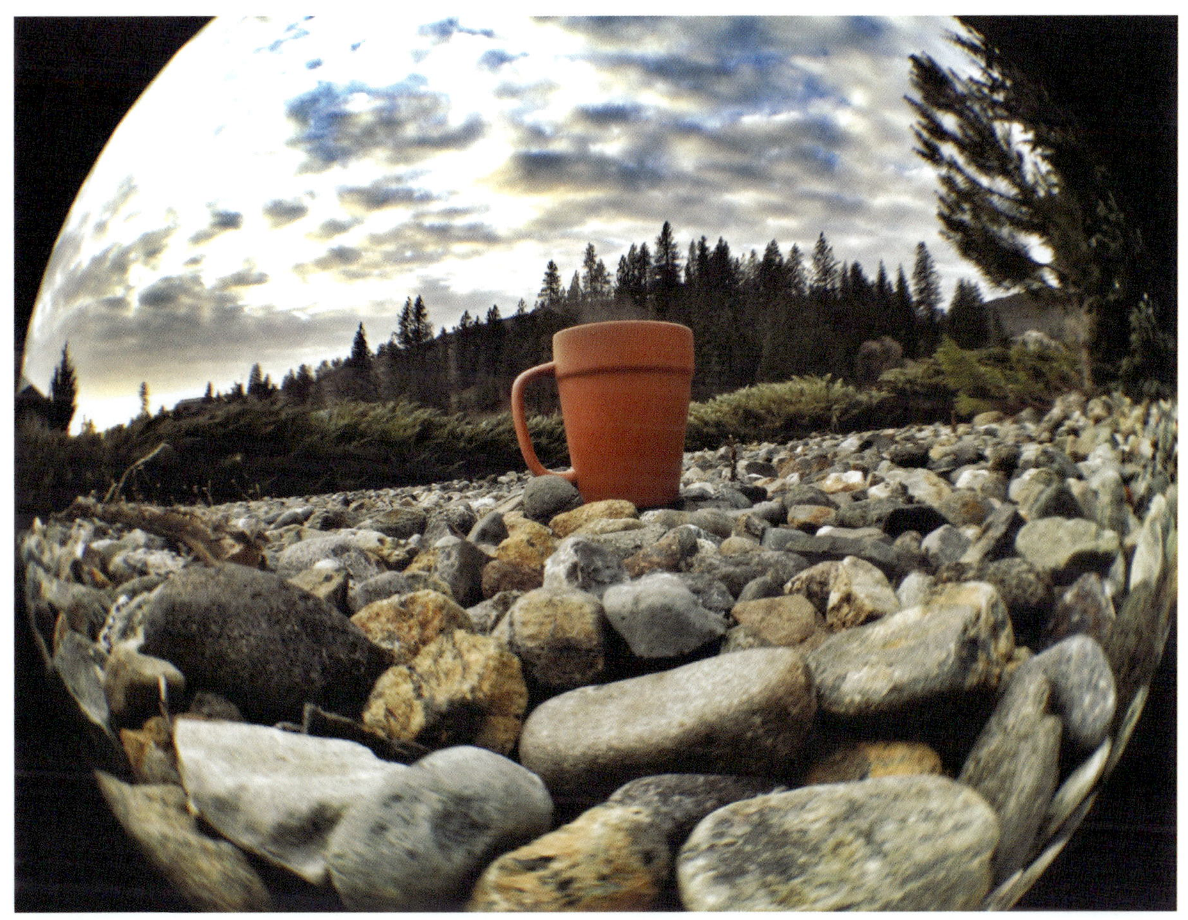

Zen garden.

Over the years, I've learned to pay attention to what's in the background as I look through my viewfinder. The things that are in the background can make or break an image.

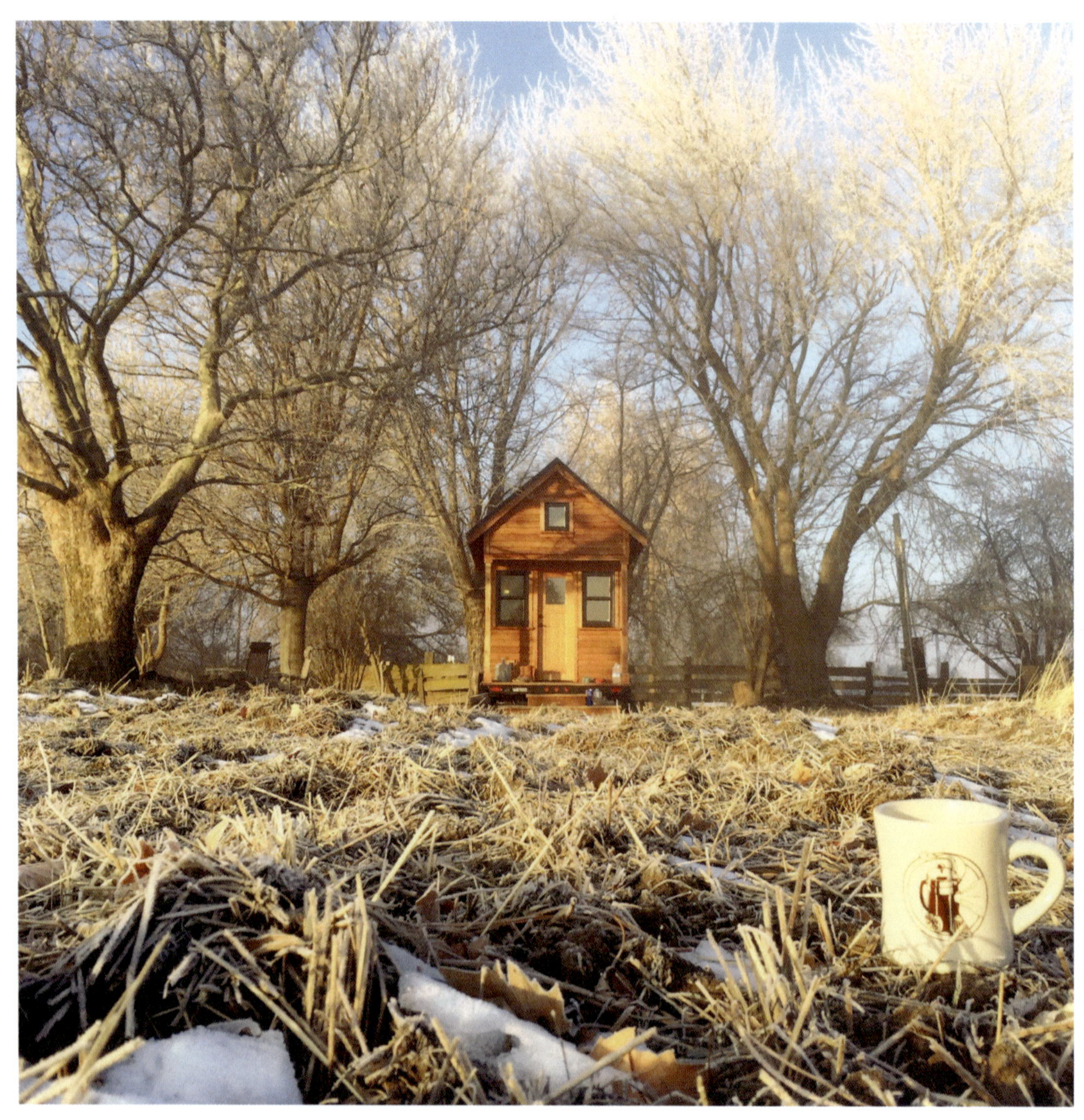

Small is beautiful.

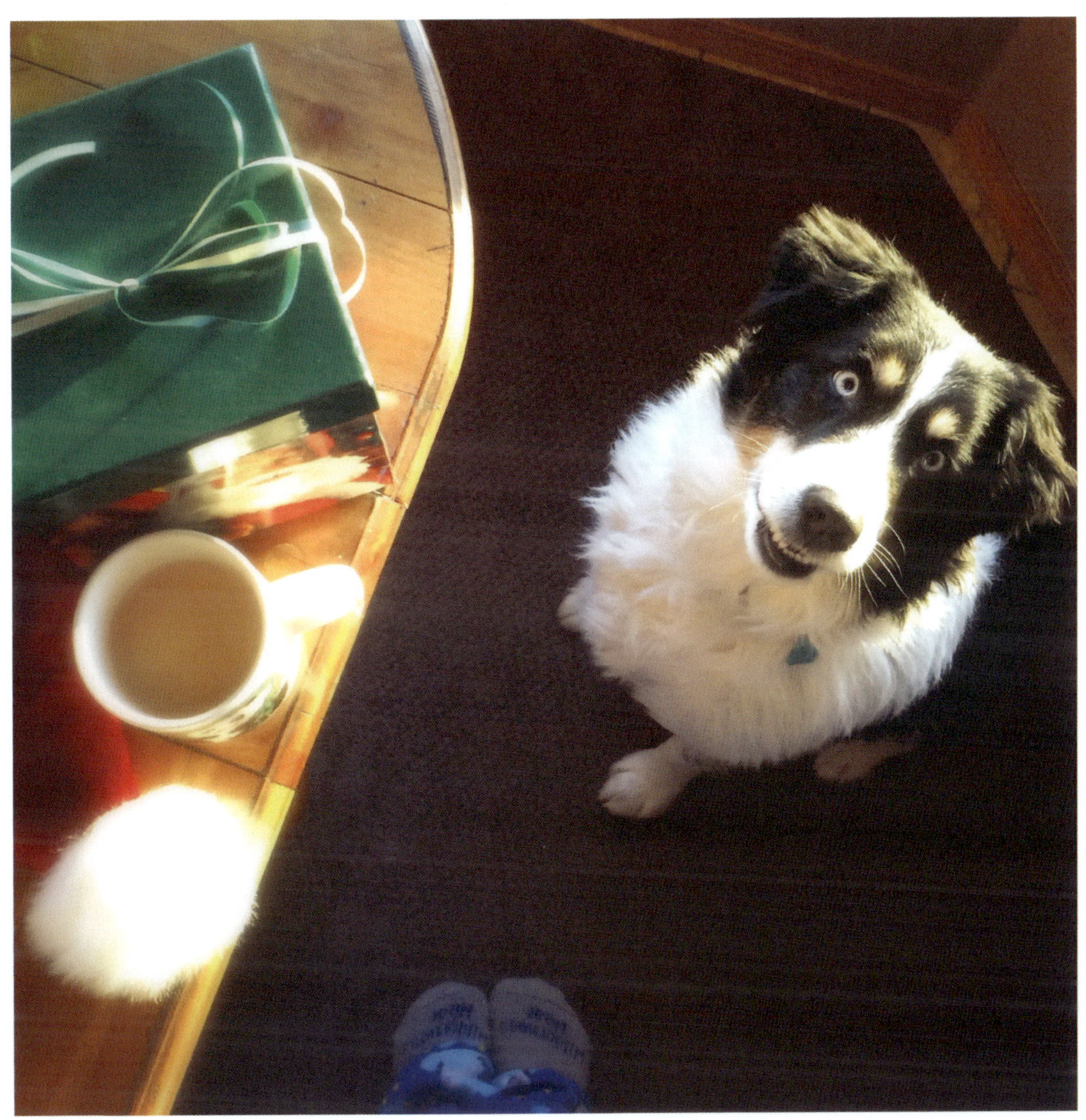

Savor the holidays.

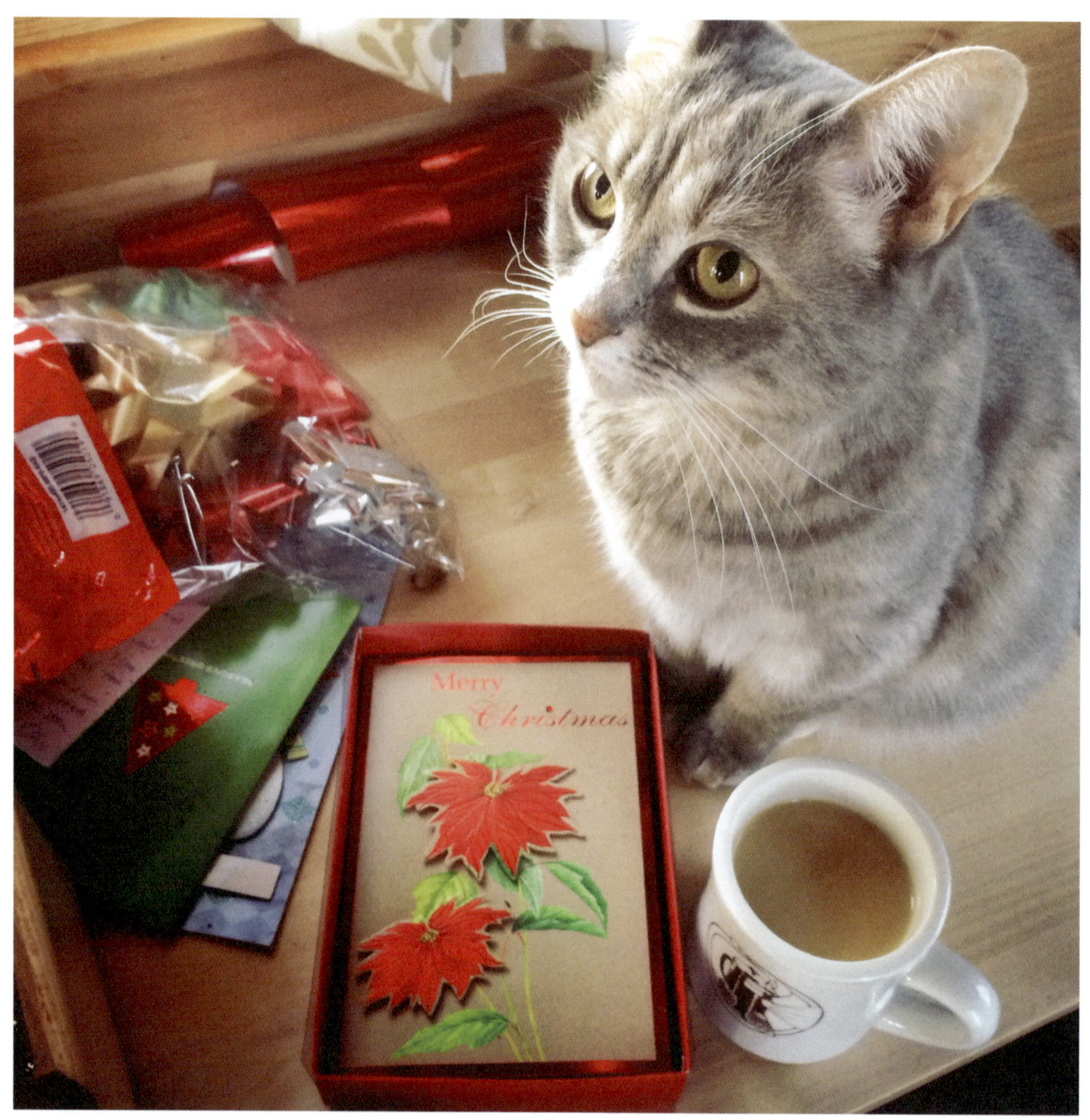
Merry
Christmas

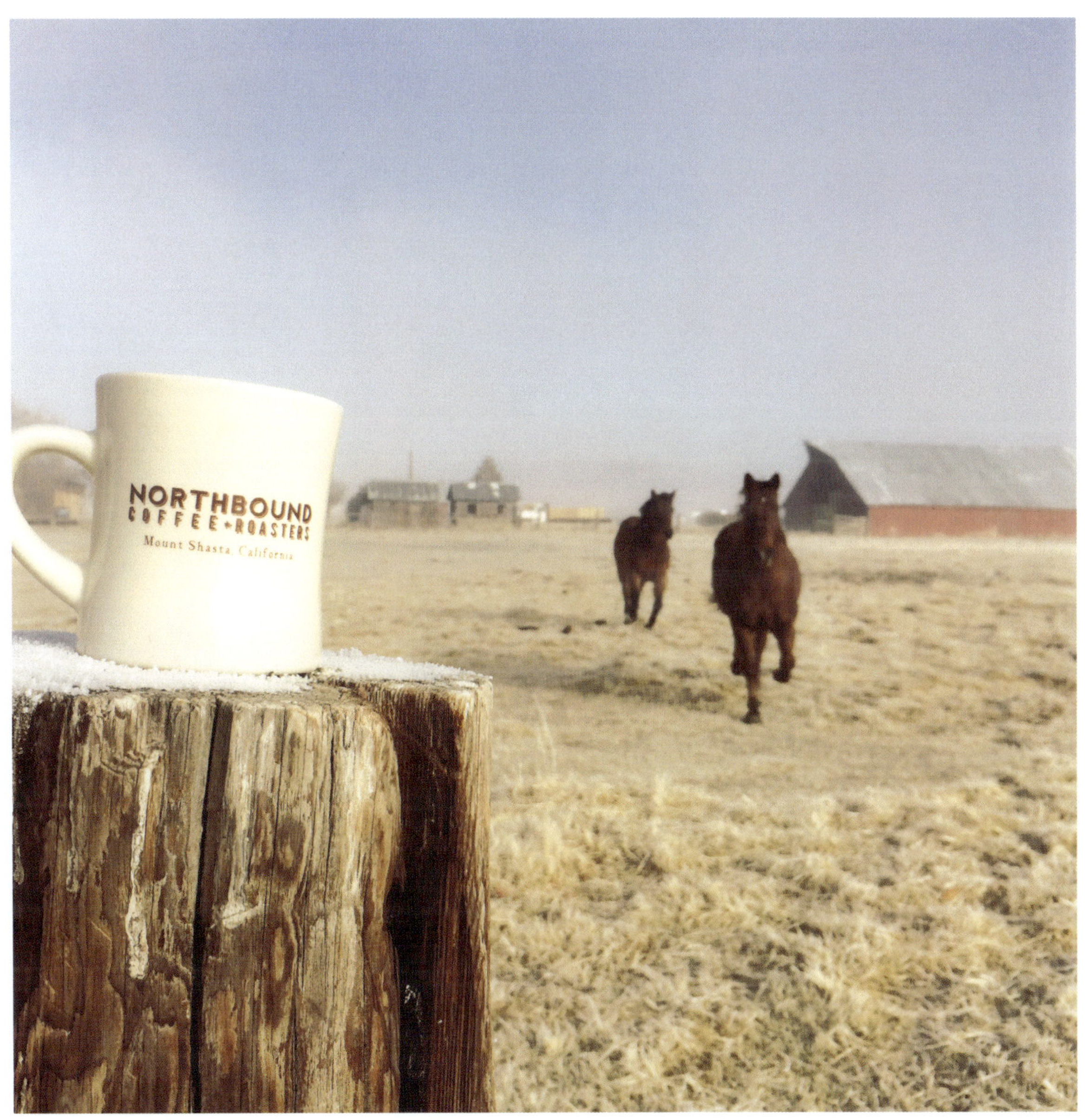
NORTHBOUND
COFFEE ROASTERS
Mount Shasta, California

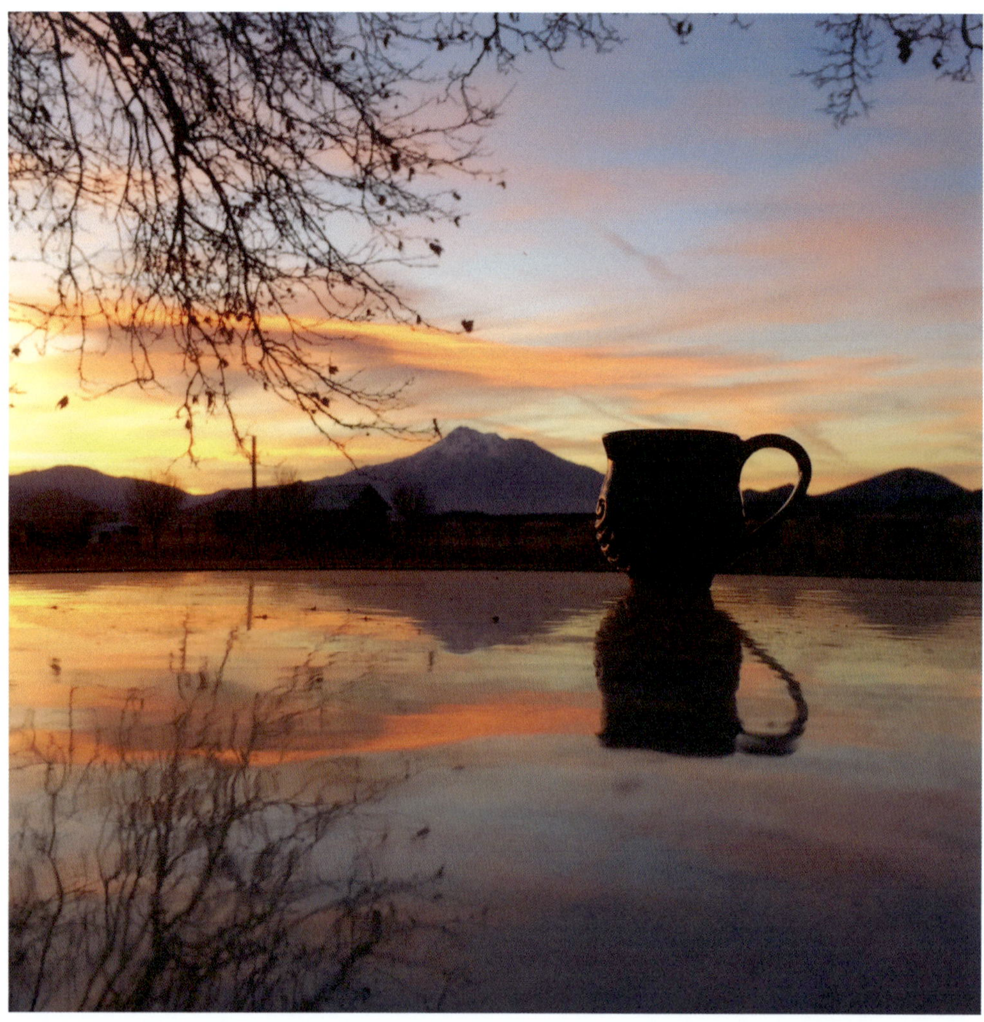

Reflection.

When you are out in the world, look around for reflective surfaces because they are everywhere. Reflections allow you to layer the image with textures and arrange subjects in an ethereal way. By using a reflective surface, you can tell an interesting story about how you see the world.

HOW TO START A DAILY PHOTOGRAPHY PROJECT

"Photography is a way of feeling, of touching, of loving. What you have caught on film is captured forever . . . It remembers the little things, long after we have forgotten everything."

—Aaron Siskind

It isn't complicated to begin a daily photography project. You don't need much to get started. Below is a brief guide to help you embark on your new photography venture.

1. **Decide to start.** The hardest part of developing a creative project is making the decision to begin. It requires time, creative energy, and the willingness to overcome your fears. When I started *My Morning View* photography series, I was scared. I was scared of what people would think, and I was fearful my iPhone photos would be horrible. Instead of focusing on my fears, I pushed past them and kept snapping pictures. Along the way, I learned a lot about photography and myself. I'm thankful I decided to start this project.

2. **Use the camera you already own.** You don't need to buy a fancy camera to begin taking pictures or to start a photography project. You can take gorgeous photos with the camera you already own,

whether it's an iPhone, a point-and-shoot, or a DSLR. Use the camera you have and understand how it works before you buy something new.

3. **Engage in deliberate practice.** My photographic voice is based on how I see the world, the type of camera I use, and how I edit my images. However, I didn't find my voice until I made the decision to engage in a ritual of daily, deliberate practice. I set aside time each morning to take photos, and it has become an ingrained part of my daily routine. I get up, make coffee, and take snapshots with my iPhone. My aim is to capture scenes that inspire me and share those images with others.

4. **Share your images.** As a kid, I loved the anticipation of dropping off my film to be processed and was always amazed when I stopped by Kmart to pick up my new pictures. I loved the feeling the pictures conveyed and how the images transported me to a different time and place. I loved—and still love—snapping pictures of my four-legged friends and the people in my life. More than anything, I adore sharing my images with family members and my online community. As you delve into your photography project, I recommend sharing your photos online. Sharing my photos on my blog and on social networks, like Instagram, is how I developed a community of peers. I'm constantly inspired by work I see online, and it makes me want to become even better at my craft. In addition, sharing my images is a wonderful way to receive positive feedback and encouragement.

And last but not least—have fun! We all see the world differently, so how you capture images depends on your perspective. I think this is where the magic lies. We all have different experiences, and those experiences color the world we live in and how we use our camera.

GRATITUDE

Acknowledging the good that you already have in your life is the foundation for all abundance.

—Eckhart Tolle

Words can't express how much I love Mahlon and how he impacted my life for the better. His guidance and support made me a better daughter, friend, wife, and photographer. Mahlon can't savor a cup of coffee at sunrise with me anymore, but I know he is still watching over me. He will always be by my side.

I'm thankful for my mom, Kathy Hettick. Like Mahlon, she has always supported my crazy ideas and dreams. I'm grateful she is part of my everyday life.

I'm also grateful for my amazing in-laws and neighbors, Roy and Cindy Smith. Our tiny house has been parked on their land since September 2012. The land is beautiful and it is the perfect spot to take thousands of photos. We moved away briefly during the summer of 2013 but soon returned. Siskiyou County is an undiscovered gem in California, and I love living here.

Soon after we moved to Siskiyou County, I discovered Northbound Coffee Roasters. Northbound Coffee is based in Mt. Shasta and their organic coffee is delicious! In my humble opinion, it is the best-tasting coffee in northern California. This coffee has fueled countless photo sessions, and it has helped me endure bitterly cold days.

I'm indebted to my friends Chris O'Byrne and Courtney Carver. If it weren't for their encouragement, I would have given up on this project. If you need a good editor, make sure you contact Chris and his awesome team at jetlaunch.net. And be sure to visit Courtney's website, bemorewithless.com.

A big "thank you" goes to my best friend and husband, Logan Smith. He puts up with my incessant photo snapping and has always encouraged my photography interests even when I want to throw my camera out the window.

And last but not least, a huge "thank you" goes to the readers of my blog rowdykittens.com. I appreciate every email and blog comment that comes my way, and I'm grateful for your continued support. I couldn't do this work without you.

With gratitude,

Tammy

ABOUT TAMMY

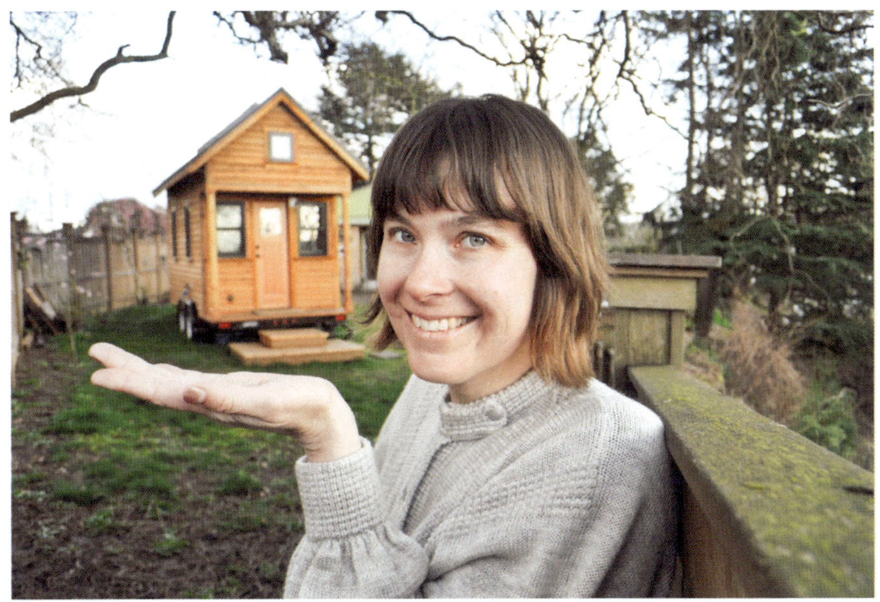

Tammy Strobel is a writer, photographer, and teacher. She created her blog, RowdyKittens.com, in late 2007 to improve her writing and to share her story. Blogging consistently improved her writing and resulted in a book deal. Tammy's first print book, *You Can Buy Happiness (and It's Cheap): How One Woman Radically Simplified Her Life and How You Can Too*, was published in September 2012. Her work has been featured by the *New York Times*, *USA Today*, the *TODAY Show, CNN, MSNBC*, and a variety of other media outlets.

Tammy spends her free time taking photos, walking, and hanging out with friends and family. She currently lives in a very tiny house in northern California, with her husband, Logan, and two cats. You can sign up for Tammy's e-courses or purchase her book at rowdykittens.com.

22567871R00054

Printed in Poland
by Amazon Fulfillment
Poland Sp. z o.o., Wrocław